THE
AMAZING CAREERS
OF
BOB HOPE

FROM GAGS TO RICHES

THE
AMAZING CAREERS
OF

FROM GAGS TO RICHES

by

JOE MORELLA

EDWARD Z. EPSTEIN

and

ELEANOR CLARK

ARLINGTON HOUSE
New Rochelle, N.Y.

DEDICATION

*To our families and, most
especially, Patrick B. Clark*

ACKNOWLEDGMENTS

Bill Faith
Ray Seery
Judy Storey (USO)
Jerry Rayboy
Allan Kalmus
Sid Eigis (NBC)
Ellis Nasseur
Kurt Bloch (NBC)

Special thanks to Bob Hope.

Library of Congress Catalog Card Number 73-10745

ISBN 0-87000-191-4

Manufactured in the United States of America

CONTENTS

Portrait of Hope, circa 1965

BIOGRAPHY

America's leading laughman and, no doubt, its richest, Bob Hope was not born into poverty in Eltham, a London suburb, on May 29, 1903. But his family—a stonemason father, an indomitable Welsh mother and four brothers (two younger brothers were yet to be born)—soon acquired it.

There were a number of factors responsible for the quick decline in the family's fortunes, but the prime one was Hope's breadwinner Dad, William Henry. The senior Hope was blessed with a zest for the good life. At times that "sans souci" air rivaled the lusty mirth of an upper-class gentleman.

His manner was men's club. He was well spoken, intelligent, convivial and lively; a happy, contented man to whom life had been generous. His honest labors as a stonecutter and a builder of middle-class homes had rewarded him with a comfortable prosperity.

But suddenly, his age, the golden age of the Victorian Empire, passed; he did not. His skill, architectural stonecarving, once had commanded top salary. The century turned, however, and the ornate style of architecture turned with it. The day of the stonemason ended. The day of the bricklayer began. The demand for Hope Sr.'s unique and old world talent dropped sharply. And the happy family homestead, a row house built by Grandfather Hope, became a tense and bittersweet abode.

William Henry Hope was an avid reader of history with a ready knowledge of the idylls of his kings. He also possessed a devotion to improving the breed. It was this love for the sport of kings, his son, Bob, later said, that made him a near pauper. And made the family desperate.

Hope has recalled his father as an artisan who, unfortunately, was as gifted with a pint of ale as with a mallet and a chisel and a piece of

7

hard rock. Although stonecarving construction jobs were drying up, William Henry seemed to be doing the opposite, trading his place on the scaffold for a spot at the bar.

When Bob Hope was about two years old, the family moved to Bristol in the hope stonemason work could be found there. But building jobs continued to be scarce. The next year Hope's father decided to join two of his brothers in America and seek a better life.

Brothers Fred (a steamfitter) and Frank (a plumber) were settled in Cleveland with their families. William Henry arrived in 1906, went to work with a vengeance, saved thriftily and sent for his brood the next year.

In the blustery March of 1908, six Hope sons and their dynamic mother, whom they addressed as "Ma'am," landed in New York after crossing the Atlantic in steerage. George, Hope's youngest brother, was born an American. Their first stop was Ellis Island and an interview with the immigration authorities. And then came a reunion in Cleveland. The families doubled up until Mrs. Hope found rooms on Standiforth Court.

Despite the proximity of his brothers, Hope Sr. never developed a fondness for the American way of life. He preferred a well-ordered world populated by his kind of men. He once mused: "The United States is a fine place for women and dogs. It's a poor place for horses and men." Hope has acknowledged that his father was an old world man in a tough new world where being brave wasn't enough.

William Henry continued to take solace in liquor. His frequent business setbacks and his drinking placed the burden of family responsibility in the lap of Hope's remarkable mother, the former Avis Townes, the daughter of a Welsh sea captain. She was a petite woman with short brown hair and brown eyes that reflected her fierce determination to help her sons carve a place in society. She had a heightened sense of ethics, tremendous energy and an unbreakable spirit. She was a font of optimism in a well of misfortune. She encouraged, she complimented, she advised and she prodded. In the dark days, she walked on the bright side of life. While her husband kept his distance from his sons, she held them close to her heart. She was a skilled and wise mother; each son believed himself to be her favorite.

In the wake of the depression of 1907 she began to take in boarders. The modest venture paid the bills and kept bread on the table. For several years the Hope household made frequent moves to larger quarters so more boarders could be accommodated. Since the

Portrait of Hope, circa 1950

stakes were, simply, survival, she was quite frank with her sons about the precarious state of the family finances. They were told that income was a family affair and as soon as they were able, the seven Hope sons were odd-jobbing ready cash in dozens of ways.

Hope himself at one time or another was a newspaper boy, a caddie, a butcher's boy, a shoe salesman and a stock boy. He also was fairly skilled with a pool cue. He hustled his friends on occasion, but since they too didn't have much money, his earning pattern in the local pool halls was erratic and nickel-dime.

Concerning his mother's hard task in raising seven boys, Jack, one of Bob Hope's brothers, said: "It wasn't an easy job. I was taken with running away from home and Bob had taken to hanging out at the local pool hall. He was a great billiard player at 12."

Jack recalls that their Aunt Louise noticed Bob hanging out there. She told their mother she feared he would turn out to be a loafer. The news did not alarm Bob's mother at all.

Said Jack: "My mother had great faith in the goodness of her sons." Aunt Louise was told not to worry about any of the boys. About Bob, Jack recalls his mother's explanation: "The poolroom is just part of growing up. Don't worry about Bob. It's his time for finding himself. He'll turn out fine."

In these early years, Hope has recalled, it was his father who was the amateur family barber. The senior Hope was more willing than talented. But he continued to give trims—slashes really—until vanity and nerve deemed the boys seek professional tonsorial attention.

Hope's father was an inconsistent disciplinarian. He was quick to anger when the punishing mood was on him, but just as apt to ignore. Mostly, he left his sons to their mother, and kept to himself.

Given her strong personal moral convictions, Mrs. Hope's life became one dedicated to her sons. She insisted they be church-goers as youngsters, and they were. Hope had been baptized Church of England as Leslie, after a famous football (soccer) player, Leslie Townes. His mother raised him as a Presbyterian. Today, he attends Catholic Services once a year at Christmas out of respect for his wife, Dolores, a devout Catholic.

His attitude toward religion is that it is a personal matter. He once told an interviewer that he was "an Episcopalian turned Presbyterian turned master of ceremonies." His daughter, Nora, once was reported as telling her brother, Kelly, that "everyone in the world's a Catholic except Daddy. *He's* a comedian."

Hope has vivid memories of his childhood:

By the time I was 7 or 8 I had developed a fairly good voice—halfway between high tenor and soprano—and it soon became a valuable source of family income. It just seemed natural that I should sing, so, when Sunday rolled around and we were broke, a bunch of us would board a streetcar for Luna Park, the local amusement park, and begin singing popular songs. I'd sing a solo, then we'd give with a quartet, and, just before getting to Luna, we'd pass the hat and split the proceeds. Part of that money we would put aside, but we generally had enough for some of the rides and booths at the park. If we were short, we generally could pick up several dollars more singing on street corners before returning home. The net always went into Ma'am's family treasury.

Although all of the boys often deprived themselves of some little luxuries to help with the family budget, we were always repaid for our sacrifices. After I started in show business ... Mother used to appear, without telling me, at one of the local neighborhood theaters where we were playing and set herself up as a one-woman claque, determined that her son would not go unappreciated. (Believe me, there were a lot of times when her efforts were more than welcome!)

One day, too, I remember, we went together to see the great Frank Fay, then a monologist. All during the performance she kept criticizing Frank's performance and comparing it with mine. "Why Leslie," she said, "you're better than he is, and, besides, you can sing and dance, too." Mother was only partly right.

Besides selling newspapers and singing, I caddied, worked in a meat shop, as a shoe store clerk, in the parts department of a motorcar company, picked up quite frequent prizes on amateur programs in local vaudeville houses, and collected many a dollar competing in races at the then popular company picnics. Each summer all the larger concerns in Cleveland would hold employee picnics at various parks around the city. George "Whitey" Jennings, my particular pal, and I would compete in as many as possible, and, because I was a fairly fast sprinter, would pick up extra dollars by winning.

We would attend as many as two or three picnics on a Sunday, a transportation feat in itself. Sometimes one or two of my brothers would go along—for the family's sake. We had most of the local runners classified in my age group, so, when we knew there was a particularly tough opponent in a certain race, we'd make plans in advance. After the start, whichever one of my brothers was running would "accidently" stumble and fall into the good opponent,

11

knocking him off stride and enabling me to win. We didn't consider that cheating—it was just for the good of the family.

Bob's real name, Leslie, gave him some problems when he was a child:

> I had been named Leslie—after a currently popular British football player, as were all the boys—and it was acceptable in the family. But, on my first day of school in Cleveland, I discovered it might not be quite so good as I thought. Dressed in approved English schoolboy style—Eton collar, flowing tie, and such—I presented myself for registration.
>
> During recess one of my classmates asked my name. In approved British fashion I replied, "Hope, Leslie." From then on, I was "Hopelessly" to the whole school, although it was later shortened to plain "Hopeless." Needless to say, I suffered a spate of bloody noses and dealt out many in return as a consequence.

As a vaudeville performer and later as a Broadway star, Hope led a busy offstage private life that was indeed private. He was blessed with an eye and an appetite for the weaker sex and a consuming belief that variety is the spice of life.

Hope did his courting in a glamorous Pierce Arrow touring car, squiring his lovely ladies in style. He bought the car in 1933 during the run of *Roberta*, his third play. Years later he recalled this glorious time as "my heyday." He was young, goodlooking, had a flashy bank roll and was confident that no word, not even rumors, would ever get back to "Ma'am" in Cleveland.

"The girls were so thick I had to push them off of the running board," he has remembered fondly.

A co-star in *Roberta*, a young man named George Murphy, was well aware of Hope's fondness for beautiful young women with "personality." After one particular evening performance, Murphy talked Hope into making a stop at the Vogue Club on 57th Street to listen to "the new songbird," Dolores Reade.

As the pair entered the club, Miss Reade, a ladylike brunette, was singing "Did You Ever See a Dream Walking?" Her beauty and low voice, which punctuated her dignified manner, had an immediate and powerful effect on Hope. He had planned other stops that night in his usual Broadway bounce, but instead he remained transfixed.

When Murphy introduced them, Bob's first words were: "Can I take you home?" During the ride to her midtown West Side apartment, Dolores asked him if he were in *Roberta* with Murphy.

Portrait of Hope, circa 1941

He said yes and then offered her two tickets to the following day's matinee.

After the show he waited in vain for her to come backstage to say hello. He was hurt and thought that perhaps she hadn't even attended the show. That night he went back to the club to ask her what had happened. She told him she felt too embarrassed because she had no idea he had such a big part. He was a lead and she had thought him to be only a chorus boy.

Years later she recalled the incident:

> I'll never forget the first time I saw him on a stage. We had met the night before—George Murphy had brought him to the Vogue Club where I was singing—but all I can capture of that first impression was that he was good looking, yes, almost handsome (to this day the caricatures of my husband annoy me). But my second impression is intact. He'd sent me tickets for Roberta and I sat in the audience scarcely breathing. Tamara had just sung the beautiful "Smoke Gets in Your Eyes." The applause was tremendous. Then Tamara and Bob sat down facing each other, midstage, Bob straddling his chair, leaning his elbows on the back. Tamara seemed to be close to tears.
>
> "There's an old Russian proverb—when your heart's on fire, smoke gets in your eyes," she said.
>
> Bob kept looking at her. "We have a proverb over here in America, too—love is like hash. You have to have confidence in it to enjoy it."
>
> No line could be more truly indicative of the real Bob. Here is a broken-hearted girl and what he is saying to her is serious, sensitive, but with a light touch, maybe just enough lightness to make her smile. This is the essence of Bob's talent and a Godgiven one. To live in this world we must have a sense of humor and in having it, don't we reflect the Divine Sense of Humor? Bob knows this intuitively. Seeing him in Roberta, I had no doubt that he was blessed, that his personality couldn't miss.

From that night Bob and Dolores dated steadily. A short interval passed while Dolores took a singing date in Florida, accompanied by her mother. The courtship continued long distance by letter and telephone. When the separation became too hard to bear, Dolores cut short her engagement and rushed back to New York. The reunion was marred by bad news from Cleveland. Bob's mother was gravely ill with cancer. He left to be by his mother's side.

When Bob returned, Dolores was furious. While he had been away, a gossip item in a show business column had reported that a certain chorus girl claimed she was going to marry Hope. Dolores

14

demanded an explanation, and Hope managed to convince her that he hadn't seen the girl in question since he and Dolores had started dating. He insisted the columnist must have made a mistake.

Satisfied with Hope's story, Dolores resumed their romance. It progressed naturally to the brink of marriage. And then over the edge. For some unknown reason, Hope chose Erie, Pennsylvania as the site of their wedding. He has said he can't remember why he selected Erie. It was unromantic and chilly, an industrial town up the shore of Lake Erie from Cleveland. But one possible reason may have been that it was not far from home. The date was February 19, 1934.

Roberta also serves to key another flood of memories in Hope's recollections. During its run Bob lost his mother. She had been the major influence in his life, and when she died a little of him died too. It is unfortunate that she was not allowed to see her son achieve the major success she always encouraged him to pursue. Even after he had gone on the road, Hope never forgot what his mother's loyalty, faith and encouragement had meant to him when he was first starting out. He always sent money home regularly, and later, when things started looking up, he bought his parents a house on Yorkshire Road in Cleveland Heights near their son Fred and his family. Hope was thrilled that he could give them something so meaningful. He had private plans to do a lot more, but tragedy intervened. However, his mother had enjoyed the new house for three or four years. Her passing devastated her husband, leaving him empty and alone. His memories kept him alive for three more years and then he passed away at age sixty-six. Years later Hope's younger brother, Sid, also died of cancer, leaving a family of five children which the other Hopes provided for.

When *Roberta* closed in July, 1934, Bob and Dolores went back into vaudeville together in an act of songs and comedy sketches. Though she continued to make intermittent stage appearances after Bob returned to Broadway, her main career eventually became that of a loyal wife.

In 1938 Hope's brother Jack, who had always hankered to enter show biz, was asked to join Bob. Hope's option had been picked up by Paramount Pictures as the result of his success in the film, *The Big Broadcast of 1938*. Jack was in Akron when Hope phoned him to ask if he would help handle his business affairs. Jack, in the retail meat business, wrote songs in his spare time.

Jack recalled that Bob asked, "Will you come out and help me?"

To the Hope brothers such a request was almost a call to arms. Jack remembered he replied, "Of course I will. I'll leave right away." Then he promptly hung up without asking Bob where to meet him.

Jack packed quickly, jumped into his 1937 Pontiac and roared off westward without looking back. The morning he arrived in Hollywood, he decided to head straight for Paramount Studios. It was early when he drove up to the main gate and told the security man he would like to see Bob Hope.

The gateman asked whom he should say was calling. "Tell him it's his brother Jack." There was little resemblance then between the two brothers. Bob had brown hair and brown eyes, like his mother, and Jack had blonde hair and blue eyes. Jack noticed then that he was being scrutinized by the guard.

"So you're his brother? Same mother and father?" the gateman asked. A call inside the studio revealed that Bob was away.

"Bob and I finally did get together later that day and we've been together ever since." Jack and Bob had been close as boys back in Cleveland when, in one rooming house or another that their mother ran, they bunked in the same room. Hope could have hired a public relations type for his scheduling and other detail work. But Bob has always believed in famly. His mother raised him that way.

Hope has often said: "Family has always been of supreme importance to me. As far back as I can remember the Hope family was a tightly knit group, ready to stand as a unit against any threat to its security, ready to fight individually for one another in any crisis whatsoever."

When it was learned that Dolores could not have children, she immediately expressed a desire to adopt, which Hope at first opposed. But she campaigned quietly and persistently. Her insistence, coupled with Hope's own strong feelings about family, persuaded him to relent.

George Burns and Gracie Allen, Hope's pals, recommended the Cradle, an adoption agency in Evanston, Illinois. The Hopes made a visit and the acquaintance of Mrs. Florence Walrath, the managing director. After extensive interviews and the appropriate investigation, Bob and Dolores were found to be suitable potential parents. In the summer of 1939, eight-week-old Linda, a disarming blonde, was adopted. Hope's initial fears of adoption were soon allayed by his bubbling new baby girl, and within a few weeks he wired Mrs. Walrath that he was very interested and desirous that Linda, who had been named by him, have a brother. A year later Tony, named

Bob and his wife Dolores when they appeared briefly together in vaudeville

by Dolores, took up permanent residence in the Hope household.

Dolores was ecstatic with her babies, and lobbied for more. Hope was agreeable but World War II and Bob's incessant traveling forced a postponement of that decision.

Hope, as always, kept in touch with his family:

> Back in 1943, when I was in England on USO tour, I managed to visit my grandfather, Jim Hope, in Hitchin, a little town near Eltham. It was near his 93rd birthday and a party had been arranged at the local pub. Nearly fifty people—relatives and friends—were present and a program of entertainment had been arranged. One of my cousins asked if I would preside at the party as an informal master of ceremonies, and I agreed.
>
> As the program started, I stood up and told a few jokes. Dead Silence. I tried a couple of more. Another egg. My only alternative was to introduce the entertainers.
>
> "And next we will have Charlie Jones on the accordian," I said, motioning to a man seated nearby.
>
> With that, my grandfather stood up. "That'll be enough, son" he said. "That's Joe Thomas, and, besides, Charlie plays the fiddle." He got a whale of a laugh, at my expense, and after taking over my spot, he continued to get them all evening with own natural wit.

In 1946, with the war ended and Hope's globetrotting temporarily grounded, his thoughts once again turned to the pleasures of parenthood. He and Dolores returned to Evanston for another meeting with Mrs. Walrath. There was a spirited baby girl, they were informed at the outset of the conversation. Later, Mrs. Walrath made a confession: "There's a boy too." Dolores hesitated, wrestling with the thought of holding close order drill with not one but two tiny tots. Bob had no reservations, as he later explained:

> ... so, while I sat and waited, she dashed from doctor to Mrs. Walrath to doctor and back again, and seemingly couldn't make up her mind. When she finally returned to the office I fooled her. I had already signed the papers for both. After all, I told her, I was sold a long time ago on America, you sold me a long time ago on kids. I like them both, and the more I can have of both the better I like life.
>
> On our way back home on the train I was paid off. Dolores and I wanted to go to the diner for lunch but we had no one to stay with the babies. The porter said, "I'd be *deeeeelighted* to take care of them. They're the best babies I've ever seen. And you know something? That little boy sure looks like his daddy!"

Hope and his brothers: Ivor, Jim, Fred, Jack, Bob and George

Nora Avis was named for both her grandmothers. Kelly, who was christened William Kelly Francis, was named after Hope's father and his Uncle Frank, who had helped unselfishly in the early Cleveland days. It illustrated Hope's trait of never forgetting anyone who had been kind to him.

As the children grew up they developed their own senses of humor about Hope, his way of earning a living and his travels. Once, when Linda was six and Tony was five, they joined Hope and some of his buddies at breakfast. They and their nurse sat at an adjoining table.

Hope greeted them by saying, "Good morning children." Tony chanted in reply, "Good morning Bob Hope." Caught off guard for an instant, Hope walked over to his son and countered: "That kind of stuff is okay when we're alone but if you don't mind just say, 'Good morning Daddy when we're in public.'"

Like the report of a high-powered rifle, Linda cracked: "We know Daddy—We're supposed to let you get all the laughs." Bested from both sides, Hope left the kids to their cereal and milk.

Hope has always kept his family and his career in separate compartments. It has been his constant practice to keep his four children out of the probing glare of the limelight. They have seldom been photographed publicly with him and they have followed his career much like his fans, by looking.

The only notable exceptions to Hope's strict separation of career and family were son Tony's trip to Korea in 1950, daughter Linda's trip to Alaska the following year, and bit part appearances by all four children in the film, *The Seven Little Foys*.

Tony and his wife Judy are graduates of Harvard Law School and have two children: Zachery, born in February, 1969, and Miranda, born in July, 1971. Nora is married with no children. Kelly, another son, is a bachelor and undecided about a career.

Daughter Linda is reported to be the family's natural wit. Her marriage in 1969 stirred a flurry of interest and publicity for two reasons. First, her husband had changed his name prior to the wedding. He is half-Jewish. Second, the wedding reception was ranked as having been among the most lavish ever held in Hollywood, a town noted for nuptial-day opulence. Held outdoors in a series of tents, the festivities were spread over an estimated five acres. Nobody got lost, mostly because there were 1,500 guests, who ranged from old show folk pals such as Bing Crosby and Dorothy Lamour to new political pals like Vice President Spiro Agnew.

Hope often jokes about his estimated wealth and other aspects of

20

Hope and his family

his very private life. At one point at the huge reception, Hope quipped: "Rarely do I do a benefit in my own home."

His newest son-in-law's name change had sparked some gossip that Hope was responsible for the young man's decision. He had been born Nathaniel Greenblatt, but on his wedding day had been married Nathaniel Lande, adopting his mother's maiden name.

Hope also joked about the name change: "When they were talking about changing his name and didn't know what to call him, I suggested Brownblatt. But nobody seemed to like my suggestion."

Bob & Dolores's marriage, while unconventional, has endured for thirty-eight years. Throughout much of their married life Bob and Dolores have been separated for long stretches due to his hectic schedule. He has used this topic as source material for his jokes on numerous occasions. The jokes often allude to his wife's understanding of his need to travel and be away from home. At other times the jokes strike a poignant note, as in this comment made about his daughter Linda at her wedding: "I traveled five years of my life and saw her so rarely that she thought I was a gas meter man who was getting fresh with her mother."

Being married to a talented husband, who has a demanding public that never seem to see enough of him, is difficult for a wife. Though Dolores cannot participate in his public moments of great personal satisfaction and pride, she shares them later when Bob is at home and unwinding.

One of his treasured trouping moments occurred on a junket to Korea, when he was invited to spend the night aboard the battleship U.S.S. *Missouri*, the "Mighty Mo." The surrender of Japan had been signed on her decks. Hope was piped aboard and as he strode toward officers' country, with the admiral at eyes front, the sailors ignored the brass and addressed their buddy.

"Hi, Ski Snoot! Hi, Niblick Nose!," came the shouts in jest. Bob smiled and waved. Later, back home, he told his wife: "You know Dolores, I just kept thinking what a lucky kind of guy I am. Here I was, walking with the admiral but buddies with the kids. It made you feel like a real American guy!"

For Dolores, Bob's big moment became hers too. She viewed it as part of the compensation for having to share him so often.

Hope has often given Dolores major credit for maintaining the semblance of a normal family atmosphere. He attributes the manner in which his children have escaped the pitfalls of being problem

Hollywood children to her influence and her strict observance of Catholicism.

Though outwardly serene the marriage has been affected by the countless separations. They reportedly have taken their toll on the personal relationship between Hope and his wife.

She has described her feelings this way: "Certainly I wish he were home more. I'm in love with Bob and this home and family we have built are incomplete without him. But in our case we've learned to realize the relativity of time. It's quality, not quantity, and every minute counts." There has never been any scandal about Hope, though he himself once confided: "I'm no angel."

Hope has always been a firm fan of the fair sex. On one occasion he defined the qualities he admires in women:

> For want of a better description, I call it "dignified sex." My wife has it, and so have Ingrid Bergman, my daughter Linda, Madeleine Carroll, Rhonda Fleming, and many, many more. Incidentally, Rhonda is an example of another of my theories: She is more beautiful now than she was when I first met her. ... I think lots of women grow more beautiful as they grow older—among them, Dolores.
>
> But I guess my top favorites are the fun girls, the ones who love to clown—among them, Dorothy Lamour, Marilyn Maxwell, Lucille Ball, Jane Russell. I like the ones who quip back. For this reason I'll always be glad to see Honey Chile Wilder, a great girl, who was once a radio actress with me and who is now the Princess Hohenlohe. And, too, I'll always love the ones with heart and courage who went with me on USO tours *during* wars—like Frances Langford.

Despite the fact that he is now seventy, Hope continues to maintain a schedule that would tire a man half his age. In addition to his television show, he does about ten college shows a year and countless benefits that take him to various parts of the country on a regular basis.

At an age when most men are enjoying retirement, Hope reportedly was making serious plans for his Las Vegas debut. As this book went to press, the trade papers indicated the deal—if completed—would be a record-breaking one.

On his annual USO tours Hope amazes his colleagues with his seemingly inexhaustible supply of energy. Hope has always had the ability to relax at a moment's notice and catnap. For the past several years he's made it a practice to have a masseur accompany him at all times to help him relax. Another habit that helps him overcome jet plane lag, an irritating ailment for the well traveled, is his insistence upon following his own schedule whenever possible.

He sleeps eight hours every day whether his sleep commences at 12 noon or 4 A.M. In addition he schedules the first few hours after waking for the tasks that require little creativity or concentration, like answering routine mail. Hope has learned that he is a late starter and paces himself accordingly.

His career has been punctuated by numerous accidents, which have resulted from his crazy comedy routines and the hazardous locations of some of his USO tours. Generally, his health has been robust, especially in view of his incredible pace. However, in 1951 he suffered a heart attack. The incident scared him but he never had another one. For close to twenty years he's had problems with his left eye. Due to thrombosis behind the retina, Hope has only minimal vision in the eye. This problem has caused difficulties since Hope no longer can rely fully on cue cards.

Hope's reported wealth has been the subject of frequent speculation leading to rumors that he has made land buys more extensive than the Louisiana Purchase in 1803. *Time* magazine once joked: "After golf, Hope's favorite game is Monopoly—played with real money." *Fortune* magazine and *Show* magazine have featured articles detailing the scope of Hope's wealth. He dismissed those accounts and others as gross exaggerations. But the fact remains that Hope has notched a proven record as an astute investor with an uncanny eye for land values. His fortune is mostly tied up in real estate. He is reportedly the largest single landowner in California.

His land acquisitions have been concentrated in California, but he does have other holdings elsewhere. After the *Time* piece, which said he was worth $500 million, he joked: "If you believe *Time* magazine, I won't go to Vietnam, I'll just send for it."

A conservative report on the value of his land holdings estimated the land at a gross worth of $388 million. Hope reportedly pays more than $1 million a year in property taxes. A liberal report assesses it at double that figure.

However, these numbers are not merely impressive. When compared to Hope's original purchase price, they are astonishing, and confirm Hope's reputation as an astute businessman. In the San Fernando Valley Hope is said to have bought 16,000 acres at an average price of $40 per—a total of $640,000. At the time it was farmland, miles and miles of beanstalks. Today the area goes by the names of Northridge, Sherman Oaks, Encino, Woodland Hills and so forth. Farmers were replaced by developers, who reportedly paid Hope an estimated $40 million so they could build $50,000 and $100,000 houses on 8,500 acres. Hope is holding on to the remaining 7,500 acres, which some conservative estimates assert to be valued at about $112 million. It is said that Hope pays property taxes on this huge tract of about $700,000 a year, an amount well in excess of the original purchase price of the whole tract. Hope also is reported to own land in the Simi Valley to the north, plus property on the side of the mountain between the two valleys.

His financial history is rife with other examples of foresight in land investments. The striking footnote here is that, even with the finest legal and financial advice available, it is conceded that all final decisions in these business transactions are his own.

A fiscal conservative from the time he was a boy, when he learned that nobody gets something for nothing, Hope has always been attracted to the relative safety of land investments. But through the years he has developed other financial interests. With Bing Crosby he started dabbling in oil in Texas in the 1940s. Bing bought into the Pittsburgh Pirates, so Bob tried the Cleveland Indians, a baseball team he once rooted for as a youth. Hope has also invested in the Los Angeles Rams, a football team, and the Del Mar Race Track. He is said to hold stock in various broadcasting stations, but generally he has shied away from dabbling as a speculator in the stock market. He does admit owning shares in a soft drink company and RCA.

Despite Hope's reputed J. Paul Getty–sized bankroll, his attitude towards money has always been eccentric. Though he allegedly arrived in Hollywood armed with $100,000 in savings and annuities, he never forgot the early hungry years of vaudeville. His wife has often described his feelings of insecurity and his fears that the money fountain would stop flowing. Hope adamantly opposed her requests for a home of their own for many years. He preferred to live on a pay-as-you-go basis. Rent money was a necessary evil. Mortgage payments were a curse.

When Hope first started making Paramount "B" movies, he made friends with a company executive who warned him on many occasions never to buy a big house, never to "go Hollywood" and live beyond his income for the sake of appearances. He told Hope to keep within his budget because the axe could fall at any time.

The advice was well intentioned and sound, but the executive did

25

not take it himself. He was living on such a grand and "phony" scale, that when he was fired, he was wiped out. He was paying for his luxuries with his salary and for his necessities on credit.

Eventually Dolores prevailed in her constant petition that there's no place as sweet as a permanent home. She and Hope marched out to a realtor. The house they chose was modest and comfortable—it was situated in the Lake Toluca section of North Hollywood. The Hope family, which included four children, Mrs. Nora Kelly (Dolores's mother), assorted dogs and other pets and domestic help, quickly outgrew the Hope homestead. Dolores campaigned for a bigger home, but Bob, ever cautious, resisted.

Getting nowhere with her tightfisted mate, Dolores went house-hunting on her own. In what she thought was a showdown, she presented him with a list of three possible choices, any one of which would suit her and her children's needs. Hope looked over the houses and pondered his decision as carefully as a foreign emissary weighing a proposed treaty.

The decision was essentially a compromise. His wife no doubt saw it as sheer defeat. Hope decided to remodel their $30,000 house instead of risking his capital in a new housing venture.

The expansion included a separate building for the offices of Hope Enterprises (Hope had incorporated his various interests and activities in 1946) so Hope wouldn't have to run his operations out of the kitchen any longer.

Dolores got her revenge many years later. While making the film *Paris Holiday*, Hope stayed on location for six months. When he returned home, it had been completely altered:

> When I got back, I had to use field glasses to dig the opposite walls of some of the vast new rooms. I could walk a block without being rained on. But while I was getting ready to let out a financial death rattle after gandering the place, Dolores cut in smoothly. "Dear, I didn't add a single room," she cooed. "All I did was redistribute." Some redistribution. Just to give you an idea, the old broom closet had redistributed into a billiard room. She'd enlarged all four children's rooms not to mention my mother-in-law's. Even the paneled pantry now looked like the set for the crowning of a British monarch.
>
> I let Dolores guide me to my own room so I would know I was home. Years ago, I was sharp enough to leave strict orders about the Captain's Cabin: Not one piece of dust was ever to be shifted. I cling to my old drapes and slip covers like a baby clings to its security blanket. But I give Dolores due credit. When my wallet

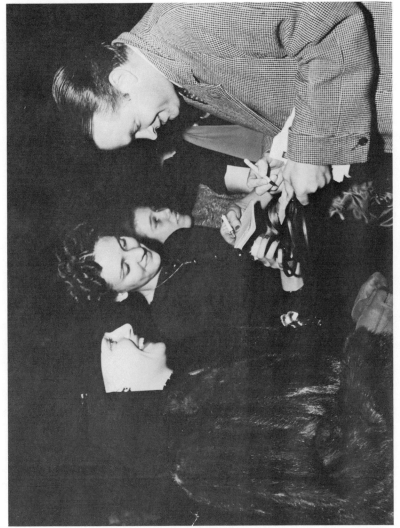

Bob and actress Ann Sheridan obliging autograph-seekers

stopped aching, I had to admit the place is quite something. I even catch myself boasting about it behind her back.

In the late sixties the house was donated by the Hopes to a Catholic religious order. When the ownership was transferred, the six acres and the two-story house were said to have a value of $1.4 million. Thus, in a little over thirty years the gross real estate worth of the property had skyrocketed 3,000 percent.

The Hopes then bought a new house, a strictly contemporary affair in Palm Springs. In 1973, construction began on a palatial $2.5 million, 29,000 square foot hilltop estate in the exclusive Southridge section of the desert city.

Hope Enterprises is now located in a luxurious high-rise office building on the prestigious end of Sunset Strip overlooking Beverly Hills.

Hope's widespread reputation for tightness with a buck grew over the years and was alluded to in a profile in *Time* magazine. To paraphrase the findings of the article, Hope was said to be cheap.

Bing Crosby was incensed. He wrote an angry letter to the editor, which asked how a guy doing two benefits a week (at the time), when his personal appearance fee was $10,000, could be called cheap. A man who gives away $20,000 a week each year could not, in fairness, be called cheap, reasoned Bing.

Time's editors replied at the bottom of Crosby's letter: "*Time* magazine agrees with Bing; however, Bob from time to time has been known to put undue pressure on a nickel," was the response.

If time is money, then Hope's attitude toward it is truly bizarre.

Hope is a tireless performer for worthy benefits. And always has been. During his early days on Broadway, Hope, a relative new-comer, was a regular performer at benefits for needy colleagues. Although many of his public gestures have caught the attention of the media, most of his private gestures have not. At least not at the time they were made.

A fairly typical example became public in October, 1972, upon the death of onetime vaudeville performer Lew Parker. The *New York Times* obituary noted an anecdote of how Parker had always been grateful for an act of pure generosity in his behalf by Bob Hope. In 1933 Parker was a young hopeful trying to crack vaudeville. He had met Hope and they became friends. While Bob was appearing in *Roberta*, he lent Parker his vaudeville material, and Parker was able to get a job.

Hope at his favorite game

Ray Seery, a New Jersey resident who occasionally writes for Hope, remembers his first encounter with the star. Seery, a serviceman, had written a fan letter to Hope asking for an autographed picture and a copy of the just published book, *I Never Left Home*. Seery enclosed money for both items. Hope promptly filled both requests and returned the money.

On the other hand, some of Hope's attitudes toward money are difficult to understand, considering his financial status. Working with his radio writers at his home in the 1940's, Hope was known to have suggested they break for dinner at a hamburger drive-in down the street. Hope's writers are without a doubt among the highest paid, if not *the* highest, in the business. His gag-writing payroll is said to total close to $750,000 a year. The salaries are high and so are the standards. Hope demands almost total dedication. It is not unusual for a writer to receive a call from Hope in the middle of the night. He has summoned his writers to Europe on a moment's notice. When the script got scrambled when Hope was filming *Paris Holiday* on location with Anita Ekberg, an emergency NAFT call was made to America. NAFT means "Need a few things now."

He has also demonstrated that no matter what, he likes his writers near at hand. Years ago, during filming of a Hope movie, writer Mel Shavelson, who was to be married during shooting, asked Hope for some time off for a honeymoon.

Hope replied: "All right. Take tomorrow afternoon off."

Two other Hope writers, Norman Panama and Melvin Frank, once felt confident enough about the material they had been submitting to audaciously ask Hope for $25-a-week raise. He turned them down flat. They quit. Years later he hired them back and paid a premium dollar to persuade them to rejoin his writing team.

In addition to his staff of eight writers Hope gathers material from part-time freelance writers across the country.

There is one trait of Hope's on which everyone agrees: he is a man of fantastic loyalty. Many of the people that surround him, from his traveling buddies (the media refer to them as companions) to his top writers have been with him for many years. Writer Norman Sullivan has been with Hope since 1938. Other aides, like Frank Liberman, one of Hope's press agents, also started getting paychecks from him in the 1930s.

In the fall of 1972, Hope answered an SOS from his oldtime radio sidekick, Honey Chile Wilder, a beautiful and witty woman who is how a society matron in Macon, Georgia. Hope flew to Macon, did a benefit and helped save the Macon Opera House.

An old friend, to Hope, is usually a best friend. Vaudeville buddy Charlie Cooly, who once fixed it so Hope got an emcee date back in Cleveland in his early desperate days as a single, is part of the Hope entourage. Barney Dean, another vaudeville pal, was always included in the retinue, until his death.

Bing Crosby and Hope, however, have two different social speeds and do not have a close social relationship. But the two invariably respond to charity events and the like.

Dorothy Lamour and Hope have always remained close friends. Dorothy and her husband Bill Howard are frequently seen in his company. Jerry Colonna, who was Hope's comedy right arm in radio, is also a close friend. He has made numerous USO tours with Hope.

Considering the degree of unselfishness of which Hope has been capable, it's not surprising that his generous accessibility to civic, charitable and humanitarian causes has resulted in a blizzard of awards. His official fact sheet places the number at nearly a thousand awards and citations.

Among these are the Medal of Freedom from President Johnson; the Congressional Gold Medal from the late President Kennedy; the People to People Award from the late President Eisenhower; the Medal of Merit from the U.S. Government; the Peabody Award; a special Oscar and the Jean Hersholt Award; the Screen Producer's Milestone Award; the IRTS Gold Medal Award; Philadelphia's Poor Richard Award; plaques for war bond service; the USO Silver Medal of Merit; Army, Navy and Air Force Awards (he considers the West Point Sylvanus Thayer Award his highest honor) the Murray-Green AFL/CIO Award; the NAB Distinguished Service Award; and the Tom Dooley Award.

Also: the Pacem in Terris Award; an Emmy; the First Honorary Membership in Harvard's Hasty Pudding Theatricals; the Herbert Hoover Memorial Award; the first AGVA Entertainer of the Year Award; the first NATO Walt Disney Award; the first Freedom Through Knowledge Award from NASA; the U.S. Navy's Distinguished Service Award; and the first Man of Humanity Award from Little League Baseball.

He holds nineteen honorary degrees, eleven of them Doctor of Humane Letters, one being from Whittier College, President

Richard Nixon's alma mater.

One of Hope's finer hours and treasured memories was the night he was "roasted" by the Friars in 1953. Accounts of the dinner marked it as one of the most memorable "celebrity nights" (the most important roast) since the club's founding. NBC taped the festivities and aired an edited version the following night. The guest list ranged from Bishop Fulton Sheen to financier Bernard Baruch. Nineteen fifty-three was a big and busy year for Hope professionally; and during it he also served as president of the American Guild of Variety Artists.

Aside from longevity, there is one other intriguing aspect of Hope's comic career that seals it as unique—his role as court jester to the president. He has hurled amiable insults in the direction of Franklin D. Roosevelt, Harry S. Truman, Dwight D. Eisenhower, John F. Kennedy, Lyndon B. Johnson and Richard M. Nixon.

Referring to the taciturn Calvin Coolidge, Hope has claimed: "I talked to him, but he never answered."

On three occasions he has assumed the same role before the crowned heads of England, the country of his birth. In 1947 he appeared before King George VI. The monarch's daughter, Queen Elizabeth II, hosted Hope in 1953 and 1955.

His popularity at the White House, unmatched by any other American comedian, has become a political tradition in the republic, it would seem. The secret lies in Hope's public discretion. His jokes are told in fun, they are not intended to hurt deeply and they are never too personal. He never mentions the private family lives of his high-level friends. Thus, he always has been warmly received, with a standing invitation to come back anytime.

No president ever really feels at home on Pennsylvania Avenue until Hope unofficially inaugurates him with a sharp, strictly topical gaff in one of his monologues on television or the banquet circuit. On occasion, the president will strike back. Lyndon Johnson made an unscheduled appearance at a 1965 USO banquet, its twenty-fifth annual, honoring Hope. He personally presented the comedian a plaque commemorating Hope's long service to his country. In an oblique reference to California Governor Ronald Reagan, a former movie actor and presidential hopeful, Johnson said Hope was unique in two respects. He was an actor. He was an actor who wasn't running for office.

Then the president said: "And he is a frequent visitor to Vietnam, who has never been asked to testify before the Senate Foreign Relations Committee. At least, not yet. I understand he was planning to testify until he discovered that there was live coverage on only one network." The audience broke up. So did Hope.

Hope probably felt closest to Eisenhower, due to their mutually fanatic love of golf. Both men frequently golfed in Palm Springs and Washington, before failing health forced Ike to hang up his clubs for a painter's easel.

Hope once commented on his friend's "retirement" from the amateur ranks, cracking: "Of course he paints a lot now instead of playing golf: it's fewer strokes." The Eisenhower Medical Center in Palm Springs is located on eighty acres of priceless land donated by Hope. He also helped raise money for the hospital building fund through the Bob Hope Desert Classic golf tournament.

In 1945, not long after he had been sworn as chief executive, Truman became the first president to invite Hope to perform at the White House. Hope did the show in front of forty Truman intimates. When Truman beat Dewey in 1948, in the most stunning presidential upset in American political history, Hope dashed off a one-word congratulatory wire: "Unpack."

Franklin D. Roosevelt was known to love a good laugh, and Hope tickled his funnybone, succeeding beyond wildest expectation at a correspondents' dinner in Washington. At the time FDR was feuding with Colonel Robert R. ("Bertie") McCormick, the publisher of the conservative Republican *Chicago Tribune*, which refers to itself modestly as "The Greatest Newspaper in America." Hope capitalized on the fact that FDR owned a dog named Fala.

"Fala has one distinction," Hope observed. "He's the only dog housebroken on the *Chicago Tribune*." The joke brought down the house. Roosevelt roared with obvious glee.

The assassination of John F. Kennedy cast a pall over the record of Hope jokes about the nation's first Catholic president. But JFK was a raconteur in his own right, a gifted and smooth storyteller who could snap off the cuff with the best, Hope has noted. At one dinner Hope says he ran off a few lines about the Kennedy clan that drew good response. But he recalls that JFK topped him easily, expressing mock shock over objections to Robert Kennedy's nomination as attorney general.

"What's wrong with his getting a little legal experience before he goes into business for himself?" the president asked.

In 1967, the year before Richard Nixon chalked up the political comeback of the century, beating Hubert Humphrey for president, he appeared at a Boys Club banquet in Pittsburgh to present Hope the group's annual Herbert Hoover Award. They compared noses on the dais to the delight of news photographers and then made a few remarks. Nixon joked that Hope had been one of his close advisers and had counseled him to debate Kennedy on television in 1960. (Many political observers felt the debates cost Nixon the election.)

Hope evened the score a few years later with a crack about Nixon's Vietnam policy.

"His plan for settling Vietnam is to let Howard Hughes buy it and move it to Las Vegas," Hope gagged.

Despite the rough and tumble repartee, Nixon remains an ardent Hope fan. The feeling is mutual. But Hope's feeling for Nixon's White House helpmate, Vice President Spiro Agnew, is much more intense. They are close personal friends. So are their families. Both men are a great deal alike; political conservatives, outspoken and poor boys made good. They share similar hard-knock backgrounds, a fact that served to bond the relationship. Both are known as men's men.

The two first met in June, 1968, when Agnew was Maryland governor and both attended a Baltimore banquet, Hope to receive an award. They sat together and discovered immediately that they were the same kind of guy. The acquaintance ripened quickly into friendship.

In many ways the friendship resembles the relationship Hope had with Bing Crosby on film in the *Road* pictures. Both men trust each other implicitly, and Hope has no reservations about telling jokes at Agnew's expense. He knows that Agnew (Ted) knows he means only to needle, not to stab.

When an Agnew golf shot at Hope's Desert Classic hit Doug Sanders in the head and made international news, Hope cracked that he was going to change the tournament's name to the Blue Cross Open. He said that the last time he had played a round with the vice president, Agnew hit a birdie, an eagle, a moose, an elk and a Mason.

Considering his jammed schedule, it's difficult to understand how Hope ever finds the time for golf. Golf to Hope is like his fabled "ski nose." It's a part of him that will never rub off. If golf ever became an organized religion, chances are Hope would join that church.

Hope was smitten by golf in his caddie days in Cleveland. He reportedly has never taken a lesson, but he shoots in the low eighties consistently. His handicap is nine.

Though a man of seventy, Hope appears physically to be approaching sixty. His voice is strong, his handshake firm and his step full of spring. Broadshouldered and six feet tall, Hope likes to keep his weight around the 180-pound mark. His ardent love of the links helps to keep his figure trim.

Hope reportedly belongs to some fifteen or twenty country clubs across the nation, so he's never too far from at least one quick round of nine holes. He is said to pay $40,000 each year in membership fees for the convenience.

His home in North Hollywood was minutes from the Lakeside Country Club, where he became a regular during his first year on the West Coast. In his back yard at Toluca Lake he had a 190-yard hole. Hope's press aides scoff at rumors that Hope sleeps with his putter, but onstage in Vietnam a golf club is an everpresent prop. Hope is said to have played on 1,500 courses around the globe, including his chip and putt pad at his home.

Hope is known as a guy who only plays to win. Someone who should know, Bing Crosby, once said: "I'd rather have him as a partner than as an opponent." Crosby added that the first thing Hope does on the first tee is try to talk his opponents out of their handicaps.

His wife, Dolores, a golf widow, has a thirteen handicap. She says she won't play with her husband again until he pays off a dollar bet they had on a round she won. Jackie Gleason, a gifted golfer who is also a skilled pool hustler, as Hope once was, says that Hope's only departure from sanity is "his insistence that he can beat me."

How long does Hope plan to remain active? Hope himself once responded to this question by answering: "I'll go as long as I can. Why, I've got a few jokes for the box. If they raise the lid, I'll say a few words on the way to the last hole." At Hope's Friars' roast, Bernard Baruch ended his remarks with an old Irish saying: "May the Lord take a liking to you, but not too soon." Millions of Hope's fans agree.

Bob Hope is unique. He has been a success in vaudeville, on Broadway, in films, on radio and on television. No other show business figure can make that claim.

His sharp-witted cracks about pomposity, politics, presidents and other venerable American institutions have transformed him from standup comic to legitimate humorist—the Will Rogers of this modern day.

His popularity continues unmatched year after year, almost as if he himself had become an institution—the warm spot in America's heart. Hope has given, and he has taken. For thirty-one years he has entertained servicemen through the USO, logging over 6 million miles by air. He also has become a multimillionaire, the richest entertainer in all of show business history.

In 1963 Hope was honored by the Congress, which voted him a gold medal as "America's most prized Ambassador of Good Will." But there was a moment early in his vaudeville career when he thought of quitting. Most of America and much of the world is glad he did not.

An early look at "Ski Nose"

VAUDEVILLE

It is easy to understand why show business appealed to teenager Leslie Townes Hope of Cleveland. Very early in life he became accustomed to supplementing the meager family budget by singing and dancing.

Visits to local variety houses and his mother's love of music and laughter (as evidenced by her purchase of a piano when there was real need for shoes and clothes) had contributed to his idea of becoming a vaudeville entertainer.

Hope found the normal nine-to-five lives led by his older brothers, and the others around him, boring. The lure of being a star and its resultant financial rewards played a big part in his decision to leave high school before he completed his junior year.

According to Hope, his first plunge into show business originated with dance lessons he had taken from a black entertainer, King Rastus Brown.

Hope started entering amateur night contests at local theatres. He won often enough that the idea of a full-time career in show business became more than a wistful dream.

Though he was encouraged by these small triumphs, he did not quit his job at his brother's butcher shop. He also took dancing lessons from former vaudeville dancer Johnny Root. At one point he actually ran the dancing classes himself and proudly exhibited cards he had printed: "Leslie Hope Will Teach You How to Dance—Clog, Soft Shoe, Waltz-Clog, Buck and Wing and Eccentric ... "

When he turned nineteen, Hope persuaded his girl friend, Mildred Rosequist, to become his dance partner. They appeared in low-budget vaudeville shows playing in nearby houses.

The partnership proved popular, but Hope still "hedged his bets" by not venturing farther than Cleveland.

It would be several years before Hope realized that his future rested on his comic talents. Meanwhile, he became aware that his act with Mildred needed some kind of gimmick.

Consequently, Hope developed the following: "This is a little dance we learned in the living room," he would explain, before the two took a brief turn around the stage.

"This is a little dance we learned in the kitchen." Then he and Mildred would dance again, utilizing a different style.

"This is a dance we learned in the parlor," Bob would say, subsequently whirling into the finale, a buck and wing. For this routine Hope and Mildred earned the princely sum of about $8.

He soon realized that Saturday-night bookings were not enough —any longer. He wanted to gamble on full-time vaudeville. However, Mildred's family was not enthusiastic about the partnership continuing beyond the familiar boundaries of Cleveland.

Hope then teamed up with a friend, Lloyd Durbin. After using several local bookings to develop their act, a date at the Bandbox Theatre in Cleveland was arranged.

The manager of the Bandbox needed a cheap act to round out his show, which starred the high-priced Fatty Arbuckle. It was 1924 and Arbuckle was attempting to make a comeback after the 1921 scandal that had forced him out of Hollywood.

In addition to a tap dance, a soft-shoe and a buck and wing, Hope and Durbin sang "Sweet Georgia Brown" and performed an Egyptian comedy dance in pantomime.

Their debut was a successs. Through Arbuckle, they were introduced to Fred Hurley, a producer of tab shows. At Arbuckle's request, Hurley found a spot for them in Hurley's *Jolly Follies*.

During this time, vaudeville was struggling to survive. Radio and motion pictures and the changing public taste in entertainment had already brought about major changes in vaudeville and its format.

Small-time vaudeville houses were rapidly disappearing and were being replaced by huge theatres equipped for both motion pictures and live performances. However, the small houses outside the big cities, especially in the midwest, continued to offer a version of old-time vaudeville by presenting "tabs"—musical and comedy tabloids.

These theatres could not afford the high salaries demanded by top-notch vaudeville talent. The tired vaudeville acts they could afford did little for the box office. However, tabs were a popular novelty, and at ten-, twenty-, thirty-cent scale some houses grossed

Hope in his vaudeville days

more with them than they did with traditional road shows at $1.50 scale.

A typical tab show lasted from eighty to ninety minutes. Instead of the standard variety format, which featured several entertainers in individual performances, tab shows were performed by a traveling company. The entire troupe usually received about $700 weekly. The typical company included approximately five entertainers and seven or eight chorus girls.

There were two types of tab show—full scale, which utilized complete plots, and bit tabs, which consisted of quick sketches. The bit tab used the technique of blacking out the stage to signal the end of a skit.

As Hope and Durbin soon learned, tab show life was grueling. Budgets were low and travel schedules hectic. From Cleveland the show trouped south by bus through several states, and eventually played houses in South Carolina.

Along the way were cheap hotels and rooming houses. Bed was often a bus seat. It wasn't the big time, but townsfolk in Brazil, Indiana; Morgantown, West Virginia; and Orangeburg, South Carolina didn't know the difference and didn't care.

That first year on the tab circuit Hope earned $40 a week. Thrifty even then and ever loyal to home, he sent half of it back to Cleveland.

In less than a year the act ended abruptly and tragically. In Huntington, West Virginia, Durbin ate a dessert of coconut cream pie. Later he complained of stomach cramps. The local doctor ordered Durbin to be rushed back to a Cleveland hospital.

There, his stomach was pumped, but it was too late. He died of food poisoning.

Hope then teamed up with George Byrne. The pair polished their routine and began to win good notices.

One of the advantages of a tab show was that it provided an entertainer with opportunities to develop his versatility. Hope was required to do more than his routines with Byrne. He also sang in the quartet, played juvenile leads in skits and appeared in small character parts.

As they gained experience, Hope and Byrne became more confident. And more ambitious. They realized they needed to broaden their appeal. The idea to expand the act was based on the fact that song-and-dance men, during this period, occupied the lower rungs of the vaudeville pecking order (they had in previous years

40

Bob and his first dancing partner, Mildred Rosequist

been the headliners). Now, however, the featured attraction was usually a two-man "talking" act. Hope and Byrne persuaded Frank Maley, the manager, to let them perform a straight comedy routine. They used a script dubbed "The Blackface Follies" and played their premiere performance in McKeesport, Pennsylvania. It was a memorable debut.

Inexperienced with makeup, both used black greasepaint instead of burnt cork. Their faces glistened.

"My, you look glossy," the manager quipped as they came offstage. Burnt cork takes minutes to remove with soap and water, however, the greasepaint took hours of scrubbing. Hope and Durbin swore off blackface.

However, they continued to expand their comedy routines.

In the two years they spent with this tab company, they perfected the following jokes in an act billed as "Smiling Eyes."

George would cross the stage with a huge plank under his arm.

Hope, the straight man, would inquire: "Where are you going?"

"To find a room," responded George. "I've already got my board."

Byrne would walk on stage with a woman's dress on a wooden hanger.

Hope: Where are you going?

Byrne: Down to get this filled.

In a more elaborate and sophisticated monologue, Hope, utilizing two different voices, would tell of being approached by a panhandler on the way to the theatre.

Panhandler: Pardon me, would you give me a dime for a cup of coffee?

"A dime for a cup of coffee—I'm an actor."

"Are you an actor?"

"Yes."

"Come in and I'll buy you a cup."

After two years with "Smiling Eyes," the fledgling jokesters were earning $50 a week.

A Detroit booking agent, Ted Snow, offered them a date at the State Theatre at $225 a week. They accepted eagerly. To them, the State meant a good shot at the big time.

Giddy with dreams of success, they promptly gambled away their savings before they got their first paycheck. Onstage, their luck was a little better. They weren't a smash but they did survive. The exposure brought other bookings around Detroit.

Hope as an aspiring comedian during his first years in vaudeville

They then swung east for a $300-a-week stint at the Stanley in Pittsburgh, on a bill with Joe (C. Q.) Henry and his North Carolinians. After the Pittsburgh date, Hope and Byrne felt they were ready for New York—the big time at last, they hoped.

They invested in fancy costumes for their Gotham venture—Eton jackets with large white collars, high-waisted trousers, white spats, big hats and shiny black canes capped with white tops.

After they had tryouts all over the city in second-, third- and fourth-line houses, they won a booking at Keith's Flushing. Their act opened with a soft-shoe dance. Then they took off the hats and donned paper-mache fireman's helmets. Byrne brandished a hatchet. Hope dragged a length of hose attached to a water bulb. A snappy dance number followed to the tune of "If You Knew Susie." The drummer syncopated the clanging of a fire bell. The routine ended with the two squirting water from the hose.

Hope and Byrne found that New York was a harsh place for vaudevillians without steady bookings. Hope says he and Byrne shared "the smallest double bedroom in hotel history."

Despite the regular arrival of lemon pies sent by his mother, Hope's weight and high hopes dropped sharply. He became a depressed 130 pounds.

Hope and Byrne, close to admitting defeat and abandoning New York, got lucky and were chosen for a Broadway show. They were cast in *The Sidewalks of New York*, produced by Eddie Dowling and James Hanley. Ray Dooley, Dowling's wife, starred with Ruby Keeler, Smith and Dale and Dick Keene (of the famed vaudeville team of Keene and Williams).

Sidewalks received good reviews and enjoyed a long run. Hope and Byrne didn't participate in either.

"Ray Dooley has something, Ruby Keeler has something, Bob Hope has something too, but you won't notice it if you sit back about five rows," said one reviewer.

The Hope-Byrne routine with Ruby Keeler, a small song-and-dance number set in a laundry, was scrubbed.

Back on the street but not discouraged, the pair persevered. They finally got a booking at B. S. Moss Franklin, a first-rate theatre featuring eight acts.

It was during this engagement that the team shuffled less and joked more in hopes of catching the eye of a talent agent.

But Johnny Hyde of the William Morris Agency flatly advised them to head west, change their act and start over again.

44

Hope took the advice and wired Mike Shea, a Cleveland agent who had a knack for finding dates for acts working their way toward Chicago from New York. Their first job was three days at a tiny theatre in New Castle, Pennsylvania. The comedown from New York to New Castle was reflected in their salary—$50 a week for the both of them.

The three days paved the way for Hope's rise and Byrne's retirement. There were only three acts at New Castle. Hope and Byrne, still dancing and sowing corn, went on last. The manager asked Hope to announce coming attractions at the conclusion of their by now rather stale routine.

Hope used this opportunity to work alone to good advantage, since he had been working on his own jokes anyway: "Ladies and gentlemen. Next week Marshall Walker will be here with his 'Big Time Review.' Marshall is a Scotsman. I know him. He got married in the backyard so the chickens could get the rice."

The laughs were quick and warm. The next show Hope received an even better response. The manager told him to keep it up and Hope enlarged his "coming attractions" routine to five minutes of quips.

Later, a guy in the band gave Hope some advice: "Your double act with that dancing and those corny jokes, that's nothing. You ought to be a master of ceremonies."

Hope related the remark to Byrne. They had a long talk and George decided to hang up his shoes. Hope was on his own.

Hope headed back to Cleveland and a booking on a rotary circuit, which consisted of one-night stands all over the city.

Once again it was Mike Shea who kept the stage door open for Hope.

As a single, the young comedian developed a routine that borrowed heavily from his past experience. Using burnt cork this time, he became a blackface comic dressed in cotton gloves, a tiny derby hat and a big red bow tie. Blackface comedians were a peculiar breed, even for vaudeville. The tradition had originated with oldtime minstrels who used blackface to create a character; but blackface had become so common in the later years of vaudeville that it was not unusual for Jewish, Italian and other ethnic jokes to be told, with appropriate dialects, while the comic was in blackface. Blackface, accompanied by other adornments such as a funny hat or oversized shoes, was used as a signal to alert the audience that something funny was about to come.

With old material and new jokes he picked up along the way, Hope wisecracked a bit and then encored with a song and dance.

Within a few weeks Hope abandoned blackface. The decision was made through necessity. One evening he missed the streetcar and arrived at the theatre too late to apply the cork. He was surprised to find that audiences liked him better without the makeup.

"Don't ever put that cork on again," joked Mike Shea. "Your face is funny the way it is."

Despite the slighting allusion to his looks, Hope recognized good advice.

After many appearances in Cleveland as a single, Hope felt he had gained enough experience and confidence to tackle Chicago. But he couldn't secure a booking. He changed his name from Leslie to Lester, feeling that the new name sounded more masculine. He was $400 in debt and thought seriously about packing it in and going home.

But a friend from his school days, Charlie Cooly, bailed him out. Cooly introduced him to Charlie Hogan, the man responsible for booking acts for many theatres around Chicago.

Hogan got Hope three days at the West Englewood Theatre. Salary: $25 per appearance. He wasn't a smash but succeeded in impressing the manager. From the West Englewood he went on to the Stratford.

During this period it wasn't unusual for a theatre to have a regular emcee. Other acts would change, but an emcee who drew a good following at a particular theatre would become a regular attraction.

The emcee at the Stratford had made a lot of fans but he had also become difficult to handle. He had been fired and the theatre still had not found an adequate replacement.

Hope proved more than adequate. His first night a success, he was asked to stay on for two more weeks. The engagement stretched into six months at the salary of $300 a week.

There were advantages to the extended run at the Stratford beside the steady pay. Because of the constant exposure to essentially the same audience, jokes became stale overnight. Hope was forced to develop new material.

A great many in the audience attended at least twice a week. Hope tapped every source of humor he could think of.

In addition, he asked every new act if they had heard any good jokes in their travels. He regularly clipped gags from *College Humor* magazine.

Hope learned a lot about audiences during his run at the

Bob in 1935 with his radio co-star, Honey Chile Wilder

Stratford. He learned that a standup comedian must be able to control his audience. A technique he developed to achieve this control was "to wait."

To wait until they grasped the implications of his quip. He would lead the program off with a subtle joke and after delivering the punch line, he'd tell the audience, "Go ahead, figure it out."

Sometimes the wait seemed endless, but he steeled himself to let the audience make the next move. It was a technique he would use throughout his career.

Hope learned to vary his approach. He discovered it alienated an audience if a comedian came on too smart, too slick, or too subtle. Often, when he told a real clinker, he would join in knocking the pun by making derisive facial gestures, adding: "I found that joke in my stocking. If it happens again, I'll change laundries."

But the strain of having to regularly develop new material became too much and Hope left the Stratford to form a partnership with Louise Troxell. The routines they used were simple, familiar and outrageously corny. For example, Louise would stroll onstage carrying a small bag and greet Hope. He would return the hello with a query: "What do you have in your little bag?" In a perfectly reasonable tone of voice, she'd reply: "Mustard." Puzzled, Hope would then question her some more. "What's the idea?" he'd ask. "You can never tell when you're going to meet a ham!"

To make the act successful, Hope had to convince the audience that he too found his partner's gibes pure corn. With facial contortions and various hand and arm gestures, he conveyed this effectively. It made him appear to be one of the audience.

This technique, in its embryonic stage at this period of Hope's career, remains an integral part of his comic makeup. He is able to adopt a dual role in many of his routines. He is not only the performer, but he steps outside of himself to join the audience in looking on and, at times, criticizing.

This technique enables Hope to exert a great deal of control over his audience. Once having gained their acceptance and understanding, he is able to overcome poor material and still get laughs.

Louise and Bob spent time on the Keith Western circuit, considered a notch below the big time, the Western Vaudeville circuit and the Interstate Time in Fort Worth.

A turning point in his career occurred during an engagement in Fort Worth. Hope had become accustomed to delivering his patter in a rapid nonstop style that practically dared his listeners to keep

Bob and the boys in the band

up. Timing as such was practically nonexistent, since his delivery usually came at a blinding rate of speed.

Audiences had always responded well to this style of delivery; the bookings were solid and Hope never considered an alternative.

Until he flopped in Fort Worth. There, Texans liked gags delivered slow fire. They wanted time to laugh.

At first Hope thought his Lone Star State audience was simply a bunch of hayseeds, slow on the uptake. He quickly found out this assumption was wrong.

A man Hope thought to be a member of the paying audience came backstage after the show with the suggestion that Hope slow down and give the Texans an opportunity to absorb the material, one quip at a time.

The unwelcome and nervy visitor also suggested that Hope try to appear more relaxed onstage.

When the stranger had gone, Hope asked out loud: "Who the hell was that wise guy?"

"Bob O'Donnell," he was told. "Runs the circuit."

The fact that O'Donnell was the local entrepreneur weighed heavily in Hope's decision to heed the advice. The next show he slowed things down a bit. The audience was more responsive.

He continued to experiment with the speed of his delivery. By the time he played his next date, Dallas, he had solved the timing dilemma. He was a solid hit. But more than that, Hope had created a new stage personality combining wisecracks, timing and a dual personality. In addition, he had changed his name to Bob.

Fortunately for Bob Hope, O'Donnell was a man who gave more than free advice. The local showman alerted the B. F. Keith office in New York, recommending Hope as a potential star. He urged the Keith people to catch one of Hope's shows and to sign him.

Bob had not forgotten New York. He was determined to try the big time again.

He had been exchanging letters with Morris and Feil, New York agents. It was 1929 and for most Americans the years ahead would be desperate. But for Hope, 1929 was a banner year.

Unfortunately, Morris and Feil did not consider Bob Hope someone special at all. They saw him as just another talent.

Disappointed but determined, Hope met with Lee Stewart, a representative of the B. F. Keith office. Stewart was aware of O'Donnell's recommendation, but the Keith office insisted on seeing Hope's act before making any kind of deal.

A brief haggle over theatre location was followed by an agreement for Hope to accept a date at Proctor's 86th Street.

Hope checked the house out. To his dismay he found that it was not a small, intimate theatre. It was a cavern. He was chilled at the thought of playing there.

To warm up both himself and his act, he booked a three-day date at the Dyker in Brooklyn for $8 a day. This was not unusual. Comedians often broke in their routines in other theatres. George Burns has frequently reminisced about the practice of perfecting routines in Wilkes Barre or Scranton before hitting New York.

Hope figured he'd be a smash in Brooklyn. He was wrong.

Neither his nerves nor his confidence improved after that short date. In private he blamed his lackluster reception on the audience. Publicly he was a picture of bravado, even after Stewart delivered a bleak post-mortem after having attended the show.

Hope arrived early at Proctor's on the eve of his opening there. A comment from a doorman sent his expectations plummeting even further. In response to Bob's query about the kind of an audience he could expect, the doorman replied:

"Toughest in New York."

Opening night he was preceded by Leatrice Joy, the famous movie actress, who had been in the headlines a great deal because of her stormy marriage to silent screen idol John Gilbert.

Aware that the audience's overall reception quite often hinges on its initial reaction, Hope used the news of Miss Joy's marital misfortunes to pave his way into the heart of the Proctor's crowd. The picture of cocky confidence, he strode midstage, a derby perched jauntily on his head. Peering at the house, he quipped: "No, lady. This is not John Gilbert." The audience roared. Hope had them in his hip pocket from that moment on and never let them out. He brought the house down with his finale and was easily the hit of the night.

By the end of the second show, the Keith Agency had signed him for $450 a week.

Variety reviewed his performance under "New Acts," stating, in part: "He sings 'True Blue' for laughs and 'Pagan Love Song' straight—both very good."

The B. F. Keith office was the single most powerful force in vaudeville. Under the firm dictatorial hand of founder B. F. Keith and his strong assistant, Edward Franklin Albee (the adoptive grandfather of playwright Edward Albee), the Keith office controlled a virtual vaudeville monopoly in the East. It was the exclusive booking agent for the mecca of vaudeville, the Palace Theatre.

Once under the Keith wing Hope made known his desire to play the top, the Palace. In the heyday of vaudeville, Hope's idea of playing the Palace would have been considered arrogant and impudent. After all, he had only arrived in New York.

But talking pictures and radio had cut into the live entertainment scene. By 1929 the once imperial Palace was no longer able to boast "headliners only."

The Palace also was forced to abandon its policy of two shows a day. "Two-a-day" had always been the hallmark of the "big time" versus "the sticks."

The Palace, which in its heyday netted $800,000 a year on bills that cost $8,000 a week, was losing money at a rate of $4,000 a week.

The editors of *Variety* had, a couple of years earlier, foreseen the inevitable. They moved the vaudeville section to the back of the paper. Motion pictures were given star billing. By 1929, *Variety* announced: "1929 will most likely decide the fate of vaudeville as a business."

But as far as the dwindling ranks of vaudeville fans and hopefuls like Bob Hope were concerned, the Palace still meant top of the entertainment world.

Even with a Keith contract in his pocket, Hope still didn't make the Palace team. But he and Louise continued to polish their routines. The humor became more sophisticated and a great deal more complex. He began to develop a satiric tone in his routine.

For example, he would open the act:

"Now that the amateurs are finished ... "

He continued to work on the put-down type of comedy, capitalizing on this technique to win audience empathy. For example:

Hope: I'd like to see more of you. Why don't you let me take you out tonight.
Girl: No, I'm busy. I'm taking my little dog to the hospital.
Hope: You're taking that little dog to the hospital? You must think a lot of that dog.
Girl: I do.
Hope: I wish I could take its place.
Girl: So do I. I'm taking it to the hospital to have its ears shortened.

During this time Hope hired his first comedy writer, Al Boasberg, who had turned out gags for some of vaudeville's greatest comedy

Hope and his radio co-star, Honey Chile Wilder, exchanging quips

acts. (Boasberg later wrote for radio.)

This was the beginning of a Hope trademark—writers. He understood that his success depended upon a continuous stream of topical material. He realized he couldn't resort to mugging and pantomine as did other laughmen. His forte, he decided, was delivery.

Hope's dream finally became a reality when he played the Palace in a revue, *Antics of 1931*. Opening-night reviews were, for the most part, lukewarm (this would be a pattern in Hope's career). There was one exception: The *Daily Graphic* critic commented: "They say that Bob Hope is the sensation of the Midwest. If that's so why doesn't he go back there?"

Bitterly disappointed over the press reaction to his opening, Hope actually considered canceling the remainder of his engagement at the Palace. Harry Hershfield, the famous humorist and cartoonist, persuaded Hope to continue.

The second night Hope was nervous and showed it. Fortunately for him, Sunday night was Celebrity Night at the Palace. In an attempt to bolster its slumping box office, the Palace had swallowed its pride and borrowed an idea pioneered by the old Winter Garden. The emcee of the week would introduce various celebrities seated in the audience and, more often than not, stars would take to the stage and perform for free. (Ironically, Al Jolson, who had never played the Palace, made his debut there in just such a fashion.) Seated in the crowd during Hope's appearance was Ted Healey, the renowned "nut" comedian, and Ken Murray, another vaudeville veteran.

Healey had caught Hope's act at the Albee and gave him confidence with his complimentary appraisal of it. Both Healey and Murray had emceed shows at the Palace themselves, and were undoubtedly aware of Hope's plight.

Anxious to help a fellow comic in obvious distress, the two bounced to the stage after their introductions, giving off an air of breezy confidence. With the audience hoping for mayhem (Healey would become world famous when he assembled the Three Stooges), they joked along through Hope's bit, restoring his confidence and enabling him to finish on the up-side.

The double-entendre facet of Hope's comedy became more daring. A good example is the following Mati Hari routine, used in *Antics of 1931*.

Hope played the captain of a firing squad ordered to execute a female spy. He wore a sword, while the firing squad brandished the customary rifles. Hope approached the girl and asked:

Hope: Madame, have you anything to say before you die?
Madame: (*Shaking her head*) Nothing.
Hope: (*In a stage whisper*) Remember, not a word about last night.

Then, to his men, he'd order in a loud voice; "Ready, Aim ... "
Madame would then drop her coat, exposing her brassiere.

Hope: At ease men.

He approached the girl, then looked over his shoulder. The soldiers were following closely behind.

Hope: (*Barking*) Back you pigs. What do you want?
Troops: The same as you, only you're the captain.

When Hope commanded: "Fire!", the spy dropped her coat entirely. She was also wearing bikini panties, very racy for the day. The firing squad dropped their guns and made a mad dash for her.

As illustrated by Hope's routine, the censorship days of vaudeville were part of a by-gone era. It is interesting to note that in the early twenties, when Keith's could dictate its terms, censorship was an accepted part of vaudeville. In 1921, even slang expressions like "hot dog," "that's the cat's meow," "the cat's pajamas" and "hot cat" were considered unacceptable. The Palace forbade the baring of legs in 1924, and the following year performers were ordered to delete damns, Gods and similar expressions from their acts.

But as business declined so did the zeal of the censors. By 1929 even the Palace reflected the change of attitudes.

Then the trend toward slightly "blue" material became so rapid that by 1929 the Keith Circuit had compiled a list of seventy-three forbidden lines, or routines. Political allusions were taboo and double-entendre lines, like "I'm not going to show everything at these prices" or "Mother is home sick in bed with the doctor," were still considered too vulgar for the family audiences that vaudeville tended to think of as its target.

Hope continued to play vaudeville dates for approximately six years after his Palace appearance. A highlight of the remaining years was his second appearance at the Capitol Theatre in New York, which teamed him for the first time with a popular singer of the day, Bing Crosby.

Hope's love of vaudeville never died. In 1948 and many times thereafter, Bob renewed his ties with vaudeville by appearing at

London's famed vaudeville house, the Palladium. He was always a big hit with British audiences, who were eager to welcome back "one of their own." Unlike many other American performers, Hope received critical acclaim from the British press.

One London critic hailed his debut: "Bob's well known face, square, forceful and keeneyed, which has carried so many films to big success, seemed a little anxious when it first gazed at the Palladium audience, but there was no need to worry. Mr. Hope is not only a real comedian, but a real actor; and his timing is comparable to that of Jack Benny, about whom, of course, he had a gag."

In Hope's later careers, notably television, his talents as a vaudevillian were put to good use. But during the thirties Bob realized that vaudeville was doomed and that his future in show business lay in other areas.

BROADWAY

Hope had first appeared on Broadway in 1927 in *Sidewalks of New York*, with his partner, George Byrne, but his first solo shot came in *Ballyhoo of 1932*.

This piece had been created by Lewis Gensler, the composer of *Queen of Hearts*, the show that helped make the ballad, "Cross My Heart," a standard. Sharing equal credit with Gensler were Bobby Connelly, the famed choreographer who had done the Ziegfeld failure, *Show Girl*, Norman Anthony and Russell Paterson, the editor of the satirical magazine for which the show was named.

The team of writer-producers had become interested in Hope when Al Jolson's manager, Billy Grady, persuaded them to catch Bob's Palace appearance in *Antics of 1931*. The Keith office, which had Hope under exclusive contract, permitted him to do a Broadway stint, hoping it would enhance his appeal on the vaudeville circuit.

Vaudeville headliners needed exposure in other segments of show business. Good notices on the legitimate stage would help to bring in the paying customers on the circuit.

The Broadway bit helped Hope in two ways. It gave him the chance to work in another entertainment medium. And there was a salary hike: For his work in the show, Hope was paid $600 a week.

Ballyhoo featured a big and famous cast. Included were Willie and Eugene Howard, a brother act of song and comedy, who were Palace favorites. Willie eventually became a revue star, a popular singer, comedian and mimic.

Others in the cast were Lulu McConnell, Vera Marsh and Paul and Grace Hartman, and the standing order of gorgeous and statuesque show girls.

Out-of-town opening night in Atlantic City presented Hope with a sterling opportunity to demonstrate his ability to ad-lib.

First-night jitters led to a communications snag. The opening number was delayed. The orchestra repeated the overture. The audience quickly became restive.

Backstage was sheer panic. Lee Shubert, a backer along with his brother, watching his investment first-hand backstage, saw his dollars flying away as quickly as the minutes.

Plucking salvation from apparent disaster, he ordered Hope to quip the annoyed paying customers into patience. The audience was by now clapping derisively.

Running out to centerstage, Bob joked: "Ladies and gentlemen, this is the first time I've ever been on before the acrobats." Laughter. The audience, perplexed, figured Hope was part of the show.

His crack hit home for the veteran showgoers in the crowd, who knew that vaudeville acrobats were so-called dumb acts, speechless routines that opened or closed a show.

The standard vaudeville trade gag explained that "the opening act sees 'em setting down and the closing act sees lottsa haircuts." As a defense against late-comers and "spring butts" with an irritating habit of leaving early, dumb acts opened and closed a show to ensure the talking acts played in a receptive atmosphere.

With the audience caught off-guard for a moment by his unusual and unconventional opening gambit, Hope continued to ad-lib his way into Lee Shubert's wallet, which is where his enemies accused him of storing his heart.

" . . . but we're doing a new number for you tonight and we had a little late rehearsal, and things aren't set up, and this is a new show," Hope announced.

Scanning the balcony, Hope then called out a greeting, which the audience thought was directed to one of the ticket-holders.

"Hello, Sam." (Pause. Then a stage-whisper to the audience.) "That's one of our backers up there. He says he's not nervous, but I notice that he buckled his safety belt."

Loud laughter. He had the crowd on his side. They were pleased. His quick delivery had won them over. He continued for more than five minutes, spontaneous and unrehearsed. The crowd loved it.

Shubert and the production staff immediately grasped the significance of Hope's success. They suggested that he open the show each evening, using the same kind of routine.

At first Hope balked. Later, he offered an alternative entitled "The Complaint Department." Sight-unseen, no script, no preview, Hope's on-the-spot skit won approval from the high command.

The idea put Hope onstage, before the overture, sitting in a

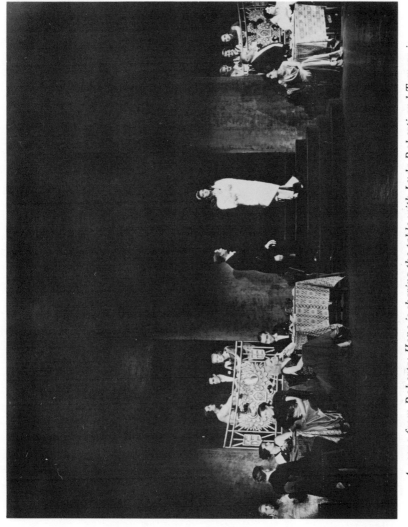

A scene from Roberta: Hope is sharing the table with Lyda Roberti and Tamara is making her entrance

makeshift box made-up to look like a department store complaint booth. The following warm-up won instant popularity.

"Ladies and gentlemen. We're inaugurating a new policy called the Complaint Department. If you don't like this show come to me and whisper your beef to me. If you tell others, it might prejudice them against our production. Also, we could use a few really funny skits. So bring your ideas to me. I'll help you rewrite them. Maybe between us we can hold up the management for some important dough."

He would continue in this vein for a few minutes. Then he would confide, "Well, I guess I've killed about four minutes. Let's go, orchestra!" He would clap his hands sharply. Nothing would happen.

Next, Hope would gesture authoritatively in the direction of the pit and announce confidently, "Take it away."

Silence. And then, barely audible, the sound of snoring. Both the audience and Hope would realize at the same time that the musicians were sound asleep. Hope would then rumble deeply. "Men, boys. Let's go." Then plaintively," Boys? Fellas?"

More silence. Hope would brandish a pistol. Waving it high he'd point it at the pit and fire one loud and shattering shot. The audience would be momentarily stunned. Their ears would ring.

When the echoes had died away, the sound of snoring again could be heard.

Desperately, Hope would display a prop cash register. Down would go the key. There would be the familiar ring.

And the theatre would be filled with music. The orchestra would spring to life, thundering into the overture.

It wasn't *My Fair Lady* or *South Pacific*. But somehow, the bit worked. Looking back, it seems hard to believe that a sophisticated Broadway audience would find such a skit amusing.

Most of the critics didn't. The *New York Times* review was scathing.

"The chief things that 'Ballyhoo' lacks are charm, distinction and any kind of theatrical allure. Of blatancy, animation, rough humor and vulgarity, it has its full share," the notice stated.

But musicals of that era were frequently just extravagant variety shows. *Ballyhoo of 1932*, a two act twenty-six scene revue, depended on blackouts, an old tab show gimmick. So, Hope's opening routine fit in with the rest of the show.

By the time the show zeroed in on New York, additional skits and routines had been written into it. Others had been dropped. It didn't seem to help. *Ballyhoo* was not a standout among the 152 stage productions that opened that year.

Neither the critics nor the public exhibited any extended enthusiasm, and the show closed after about four months. Only a little discouraged but not disheartened, Hope returned to vaudeville.

His next appearance on Broadway was in the Max Gordon–Jerome Kern production of *Roberta*. He won the role of Huckleberry Haines, the bandleader, after Gordon took Kern to see him during one of his vaudeville shows at the Capitol.

The role in *Roberta* represented an important step in Hope's career. Both Kern, a respected composer, and Gordon, a can-do producer, constituted as close a guarantee of success as the show business world of that day could muster.

In addition to Gordon and Kern, there was another famous talent associated with the show: Otto Harbach, lyricist by trade, whose way with words had proven so successful that by 1926 it was estimated by some observers that he had earned about $500,000 from record and sheet-music sales alone.

From Harbach's pen had come hits such as "Rose Marie," "Sunny," "Song of the Flame" and "Wildflower." His credits included the original treatment of *No, No Nanette*, revived with great success in 1970.

Hope got the chance to appear with a first-rate cast. There was Tamara, the distaff member of the famous vaudeville dance team, Fowler and Tamara, one of the first acts to be honored with its name in lights at the Palace.

A decade later, their friendship, a relationship begun simply between a star and a seeker, ended suddenly in tragedy. Tamara was killed in the crash of a USO Flying Clipper in Lisbon in 1943.

Nearing the end of a great career was another veteran of vaudeville, Fay Templeton. Edging close to seventy, she had won fame as Little Buttercup in Gilbert and Sullivan's *H.M.S. Pinafore*. Her high moment in the show was a song entitled, "Yesterday." It was a show-stopper.

Vaudeville veteran Lyda Roberti, the vivacious Polish comedienne, a popular star of the 1931 Broadway hit, *You Said It*, was also in the lineup.

Roberta was not all babes and Bob, however. The guys in this play about the trials of a football player included dancer and former chorus boy George Murphy, later to be a U.S. senator from

California, Fred MacMurray, later to make it big as a movie and television star, Sidney Greenstreet, Mr. Mystery and Ray Middleton. The California Collegians handled the rah-rah scenes.

During the early run of the show, MacMurray tested and won a part in the film *The Gilded Lily*, which starred Claudette Colbert. Sidney Greenstreet, of course, later gained film immortality with his appearance in *Casablanca* with Humphrey Bogart in the 1940's.

Basically, the plot of *Roberta* was sort of fluffy and frilly, revolving around a football player (Ray Middleton) who inherits his aunt's dress shop, which is located in Paris.

Hope portrayed his best friend, Huckleberry Haines. George Murphy was Huckleberry's manager. The situation enabled Hope to get off a number of funny lines.

As the rehearsals and tryouts drew closer to New York, ever-ambitious Bob was eager and quick to offer suggestions on how to improve the script. Usually, the suggestions called for adding lines to his role.

One of the better lines in the play came in a scene when Hope was talking about dresses and shirts and clothes in general.

He quipped: "Long dresses don't bother me. I've got a good memory."

The joke won a big laugh for the duration of the play's run. Even today it's funny and a typical Hope crack.

The line was more than funny, however. It also was an indication that the Bob Hope style was beginning to take shape, and that Hope was beginning to discover the type of material that would become his trademark in the star-studded years to come.

Although as Hope was willing to experiment with his own jokes, he also was tied to his training origin—vaudeville. Other suggestions he made drew on this background and reflect a Hope that today few are able to recollect.

One of his ideas was to have the California Collegians use a routine they had used with some success in vaudeville. The group would don gloves designed to resemble organ keys. Mimicking a piano-player, Hope would reach out and touch each key, and as he did so a piano in the pit would sound a melodic note.

On one occasion Otto Harbach became irritated with Bob's persistent suggestions and resisted approving one. As the show continued, Hope found himself standing next to Jerome Kern while waiting for a second-act cue. He promptly asked Kern, who gave the okay. Even then, Hope grasped that the chain of command was to be

Hope and Ethel Merman co-starred in Red, Hot and Blue

used only when it worked.

Brimming with material, Hope suggested a joke for the lead-in to the show's hit song, "Smoke Gets in Your Eyes," which was sung by Tamara. This suggestion also was opposed by Harbach. The song was a lament for her love, Hope's football-playing, dress-shop-owning friend, who wasn't requiting.

But Hope persisted. Tamara's line before the song was, "There's an old Russian proverb, 'When your heart's on fire, smoke gets in your eyes.'"

Hope's crack was the response:

"We have a proverb over here in America too. 'Love is like hash. You have to have confidence in it to enjoy it.'"

Even at this point in his career, his instinct for what an audience would think hilarious was uncanny. The new joke was instantly successful and it's reception led Harbach to admit that he was wrong about trying to keep it out of the script.

The incident helps illustrate a trait that was to be both an asset and a liability to Hope throughout his long, long career. Hope gauged the potential impact of untried material with his gut. Most of the time he was right. This confidence in his instinct no doubt helped make him the star he is today.

There were times when he would ignore his writers and flop. On these occasions he outweighed their objective criticism with his gut feeling.

The notices for *Roberta* generally were favorable, and the show enjoyed a good run—from November, 1933, until July, 1934. Hope did not fare as well as the show, especially with the *New York Times*.

Its review read: "The humors of 'Roberta' are no great shakes and most of them are smugly declaimed by Bob Hope, who insists on being the life of the party and who would be more amusing if he were Fred Allen."

Despite this harsh treatment, *Roberta* was still a milestone in Hope's career. It was his first success in show business outside vaudeville. He never forgot what the show meant to him. Twenty years later he revived *Roberta* in St. Louis to help commemorate the fortieth anniversary of the city's municipal opera. Three months later, in September, 1958, he revived the show to open his NBC television season.

When *Roberta* closed after its two-hundred and fifty-fifth performance, Hope returned to vaudeville. He had acquired a new partner, singer Dolores Reade. Miss Reade took the relationship

Bob singing "I Can't Get Started with You" to Eve Arden in Ziegfeld Follies in 1936.

very seriously. She was also Mrs. Hope.

Within a few months, Hope was back rehearsing a part in a Broadway musical comedy entitled *Say When*. Written and produced by Jack McGowan and Ray Henderson, the play was about two gusty vaudeville performers who fall violently in love with two lovely members of Long Island high society. The play opened in November, 1934 at the Imperial Theatre.

Although the show as originally conceived had Harry Richman as star, the script emphasized comedy. By opening night Hope overshadowed Richman in the show. Another member of the cast was the fabled and self-crowned Russian "prince," Michael Romanoff, who years later was pronounced a phony and then just as quickly enshrined as the most delightful Hollywood fraud of all time.

Say When was saddled with a skimpy boy-meets-girl plot, and mediocre lyrics. The only aspect of the show to be singled out for praise was the comedy.

To compliment the comedy was to decorate Hope. The *New York Times* said: "They have written enough gags, most of which are neatly phrased to put Mr. Hope in pretty good form and to keep 'Say When' on the funny side of the street."

However, the gags and the *Times* were not enough to keep the show alive. After a run of about four months, it closed.

It was two years before Hope returned to Broadway. His next vehicle was the 1936 edition of the *Ziegfeld Follies*, starring Fanny Brice. The cast also included Gertrude Niesen, Hugh O'Connell, Harriet Hoctor, Eve Arden, Judy Canova and Josephine Baker.

The *Follies* was a formula display of gorgeous girls, glittering costumes and splendid scenery. Handling the designing for the costumes and the scenery was Vincente Minnelli.

Produced by Lee Shubert, its music was composed by Vernon Duke with lyrics by Ira Gershwin.

Fanny Brice was the undisputed star of the show, but Hope won acclaim for his performance. Wrote the *Times*: "She [Miss Brice] has a capital partner in Bob Hope, who is gentleman enough to be a comrade and comedian enough to be funny on his own responsibilities."

One of Hope's high moments in the show was a song done with Miss Arden, entitled, "I Can't Get Started with You." The script initially called for Miss Arden to walk quickly away from him before the first eight bars of the number were completed.

The script then directed Hope to pursue her, lean over her

Bob surrounded by a bevy of beauties from Broadway's Ziegfeld Follies in 1936 (that's Eve Arden to the left)

shoulder and breathe deeply and audibly to dramatize his emotion. The heavy breathing and the light love lyrics lacked credibility, however.

The doorman at the theatre, the Winter Garden, suggested to Hope that when he went into his heavy-breathing routine, Miss Arden should turn and inquire disdainfully: "What's the matter? Have you been running?"

Hope persuaded Miss Arden to use the line. The bit proved to be a great success

Hope's success in the *Follies* led to his role in *Red, Hot and Blue!*, with Ethel Merman and Jimmy Durante, later in 1936. *Red, Hot and Blue!* reunited the team of Russell Crouse, Howard Lindsay and Cole Porter, who along with Miss Merman, were behind the smash *Anything Goes* two years before.

Hope wasn't first choice for the role. William Gaxton, who'd had the lead in *Anything Goes*, was scheduled to star again, but he reportedly withdrew after overhearing a conversation between Russell Crouse and Merman about beefing up her role.

Both Jimmy Durante and Merman wanted top billing. The dispute was finally settled with their names in the same size type crisscrossing each other above the title. To insure complete "fairness," the positions of the names were alternated every two weeks. Hope received third billing under the Merman-Durante cross.

Red, Hot and Blue! wasn't a total success.

Brooks Atkinson of the *New York Times* said, in part, in his review: "The ghost of 'Anything Goes' has been haunting the makers of 'Red, Hot and Blue!' to their disadvantage. Some of the old ideas try to wiggle down the neck of the new show bottles."

The book bore the brunt of the criticism. It was concerned with the search for a missing heiress, whose only identifying mark was the imprint of a waffle iron on her derriere.

Miss Merman played a rich widow in love with her attorney, portrayed by Hope. Durante acted the part of a polo-playing convict who was content to spend his life in jail. There were various love entanglements, but by the fall of the final curtain, Hope and Miss Merman are paired and Durante is jailed.

Porter's contributions in song ranged from sentimental to sensational. "Good-bye Little Dream, Good-bye," "Ridin' High" and the show's rousing theme song, "Red, Hot and Blue!" were well received at the time.

But the song that has lasted was a duet sung by Merman and Hope called "It's De-Lovely."

Although *Red, Hot and Blue* did not match the fantastic success of *Anything Goes*, it racked up an impressive number of Broadway performances before heading out to the hinterland on tour.

Hope's performance in the show resulted in his being tapped by Hollywood for his first movie, *The Big Broadcast of 1938*.

Hope and Der Bingle engaging in their customary banter

RADIO

The radio broadcasting industry and Bob Hope launched their careers at approximately the same time.

Scheduled commercial broadcasting began in 1919. The radio-listening habit caught on quickly. By 1922 there were 3 million radio sets.

While Hope was fighting to win recognition as a vaudeville headliner, men like Robert Sarnoff were attempting to develop broadcasting into a source of vast wealth. By 1930 broadcasting had been magically transformed from a low-budget musical diversion into huge multimillion-dollar networks supplying America its prime source of home entertainment.

When Hope arrived on the air waves, the basic concept of commercial radio had evolved.

The gambit of offering performers "free plugs" on the air (instead of pay) as a means of recruiting entertainment talent (needed to lure a listening audience) was refined in the true American way. In 1933 the broadcasting industry would budget more than $25 million just to pay the performers.

To the sharper vaudeville veterans, the ones with premonitions that the Great Depression was ending more than just an economic era, radio was not seen as a threat to their survival as entertainers. Radio to them was a mealticket. It was a paycheck. It was a second chance to make it.

Other performers despised radio and saw it as the prime assassin of vaudeville. They retained a fondness for the idea of vaudeville —its live and freewheeling spontaneity, its fun and its character. (In little more than twenty years, the scenario repeated itself, with radio as the victim and television as the assailant.)

The latter wiser group shared the sentiments of humorist Will Rogers, who was quoted as saying: "Radio is too big a thing to be out of."

In a decade of broadcasting, radio initially had relied on recorded music to fill its time. As late as 1926 radio was 90 percent music.

But the changes came rapidly. As it sailed into the thirties, radio became a vaudeville pirate. Too new to create a galaxy of stars of its own, it shanghaied the best of Keith, Morris and the other vaudeville agencies still managing to hang on.

Names like Ben Bernie, Ed Wynn, Jack Pearl, Jack Benny, Burns and Allen, Al Jolson and Willie and Eugene Howard dominated the drive by radio to achieve more variety in programming, thus attracting listeners and advertisers. Lesser-known vaudeville performers made guest appearances on radio shows to bolster their box-office appeal. The bigger names won sponsors with relative ease. The others had their dreams and their hopes, which would soar after a guest shot.

Success was a show of your own, a sponsor who believed in you. Hope was no exception to the yearning, but it would take nearly a decade before he landed his own show.

Throughout his long career, there were to be no fan magazine fables of overnight stardom. In vaudeville, the legitimate stage, radio, films and later television, Hope found the early going rough.

His first radio bit grew out of his second appearance at the Capitol Theatre in a 1932 vaudeville show. The show was a Hope career milestone since it marked the first time he ever appeared with singer Bing Crosby.

The Capitol was owned by the Loew's Corporation. Since its executives believed in radio's ability to develop box-office attractions, Hope was booked to appear on the "Capitol Family Hour," a Sunday morning program hosted by Major Edward J. Bowes. Bowes succeeded S. L. Rothofel (Roxy) as manager of the Capitol Theatre.

The practice of airing Sunday morning programs from the Capitol had originated with Roxy and his gang in 1923.

Bowes gained lasting radio fame by producing amateur hours that attracted hordes of seven-year-old tap dancers and hillbilly musical saw maestros.

Success came quickly for Bowes. By 1935, according to a *Variety* estimate, he was the top earner in show business, grossing more than $1 million a year for a radio show, amateur units, film shorts and Capitol management.

The Bowes-Hope arrangement provided Bob with a rude introduction into the rather cutthroat realities of radio variety shows. He was grateful for the chance to get on the air, but there were times he must have had second thoughts. The reason was a simple one. Bowes used to steal his jokes.

Bowes often ordered performers to send him a copy of their material prior to their appearance. Hope found that he, the funnyman, would be playing straight man to Bowes, who was never known for his comedy while Capitol manager.

Bowes was by no means the first to try to capitalize on another's talents. By the 1930s the tendency to use another's material as one's own had reached epic proportions. In 1933 *Variety* introduced a Protective Material Department for radio as it had done years earlier for vaudeville.

Later in his career Hope himself was to be accused of having mastered the Bowes gag hijack technique.

Years later, Hope filed a million-dollar law suit against *Life* magazine for intimating that he stole jokes. He later dropped the suit.

After Bowes, Hope continued his courtship of radio. He appeared a few times on the "Fleischman Hour," which was headlined by Rudy Vallee.

Most of the variety shows of this period were named after the sponsor, but listeners and newspapers both referred to the programs by the name of the performer associated with them. For the listener it was easier to remember a star instead of a product. For the newspaper owner it was more profitable to have the manufacturer of the product buy an ad instead of giving away free plugs by using the sponsor's name in the radio listing.

The "Fleischman Hour," a weekly show, was inaugurated on October 24, 1929. It is recalled today as being radio's first professional-level variety show. One of the show's first regular stars, Jack Pearl, like Hope had his origins in vaudeville. Radio was Pearl's second chance and he made the most of it by gaining a sponsor for a show of his own in addition to his many stints on the "Fleischman Hour."

Before Hope even had a right to yearn for success in radio, he had to conquer the strangeness of performing on it. First, there was the microphone, an acutely sensitive ear that picked up a thumping heartbeat or a nervous gulp as effortlessly as it trumpeted a Wagner opera.

The mike was a terrifying and unyielding adversary. There was no room for the entertainer who mumbled or who "aaahed" his way through his material.

During a rare moment of introspection and candor, Hope later admitted to having experienced some uneasiness, recalling:

"It just seemed too strange to talk into a microphone in a studio instead of playing it for real in front of an audience. I was always very nervous on the radio. I was on Rudy Vallee's show for awhile and the engineers couldn't figure out why they kept hearing a thumping sound whenever I did my routine. They found I was kicking the mike after each joke."

Hope was not the only vaudeville-trained performer who believed his performance suffered without the presence of an audience. Ed Wynn also expressed concern over the muffling cloak that was a silent radio studio.

Wynn had been a featured star in the first stage show broadcast on radio, back on February 19, 1922.

His unforgettable first experience in radio convinced Wynn that a live audience was imperative for good comedy. As a result he pioneered the practice of studio audiences. On one occasion, during a vaudeville booking in New York, Wynn arranged to have the theatre closed on Tuesday evenings so he could broadcast his radio show before a live, paying audience. The proceeds were donated to charity. Eventually the audience participation became standard on radio.

When it became apparent there would be no angel to back his bid to conquer the air waves, Bob resumed his vaudeville and Broadway career.

However, during the next several years he managed to get booked on enough radio bits to keep his foot in the door. He made a few appearances on the "RKO Theater of the Air" and in 1935 he was featured on the "Bromo Seltzer Intimate Hour."

The show's regular cast included Al Goodman, tenor James Melton and Jane Frohman, the talented singer whose life story later was immortalized in the film, *With a Song in My Heart*.

Hope paired himself with a stunning funny girl named Honey Chile (Patricia) Wilder, who could stop traffic with her looks, her southern (Macon, Georgia) accent and her natural wit. He had met her through theatrical agent Louis Shurr.

The show encountered rating trouble, however, which upset the Bromo people and led to a decision to cancel it. Hope returned to the Loew Circuit with his wife Dolores. Honey Chile went on to become a Broadway celebrity. Later, she would become one of

Hope's regulars on the Pepsodent radio show.

Hope never forgot these early failures to crack radio. Years later, he quipped: "The first program I did was so bad, that I got an envelope from my sponsor. But there wasn't any letter in it. Just a handful of his hair."

While appearing in the run of the *Ziegfeld Follies*, Hope also did a brief radio stint on the "Atlantic Oil Show." And then, either his luck began to change or his perseverance began to pay off.

In May, 1937 he signed a twenty-six-week contract for the "Woodbury Soap Show," which was broadcast from New York. Later in the year, when Hope traveled to Hollywood to film *The Big Broadcast of 1938*, he continued to do the show via a transcontinental hookup.

The announcer would introduce him by saying, "And now we take you to Hollywood for Bob Hope!"

The comedian's need and preference for a live studio audience led to some rather unusual developments on the occasion of the first cross-country broadcast.

Two nights before he was to inaugurate the new Hollywood segment, Hope casually asked an NBC official whether tickets for the program had been distributed. The program man said no, adding that he had been unaware of Hope's desire for a live audience.

Hope was crestfallen. This feeling quickly changed to sheer terror.

"I've got to have an audience to bounce my comedy off of or I'm dead," he implored.

He was told that it was much too late to arrange for ticket distribution, publicity and other necessary preparations.

Blocked in his attempts to secure an audience through the system, Hope improvised. Ventriloquist Edgar Bergen was broadcasting from an adjacent studio, and Hope desperately asked him for help.

With Bergen's cooperation and the reluctant consent of an usher, Hope arranged to rustle Bergen's audience. The ropes and stanchions were rigged to guide Bergen's crowd into an exit feed into Hope's studio. The gambit worked smoothly, and Hope stole his first radio show.

After the Woodbury run, Hope was signed for a show entitled, "Your Hollywood Parade," a show originating from California. By this time Hope was under contract to Paramount and the show blended nicely into his plans, enabling him to fulfill the hectic demands of a film-shooting schedule.

Dick Powell was emcee. Hope's bit was a seven-to-ten minute

Bob in 1938, rehearsing for his radio show

monologue, billed as a regular feature.

Though the show flopped, Hope was a smash hit. After the first reviews, Hope became a very hot property.

Reminiscing about this important career milestone, his wife Dolores later recalled: "He used to rehearse a whole week for those seven minutes, but it proved worth it. On a star-studded show he personally rolled up a tremendous response and when the show flopped; he didn't. He'd been terrified at first and not at all sure of himself, but within a few weeks he had all the poise he needed; the response had given it to him and I'm sure the response came because he was so refreshing—a wit instead of a buffoon."

Hope's stint on "Your Hollywood Parade" was significant for another very important professional reason. It was on this show that Hope developed his trademark—the topical joke.

Hope's monologue was based solely on the topical concept. Since the show originated from Hollywood, much of his material involved movie capital gossip. But other areas of topicality also were explored.

The rapid-fire monologue with topical jokes eventually catapulted Hope to radio stardom. (Years later excerpts from the previous night's monologue would appear on the Dow-Jones ticker.) But the monologue demanded an approach that was different from those used in vaudeville or situation-type comedy, which prevailed at the time. It also demanded top-quality writing and talented writers who could churn out a script by reading newspaper headlines.

During this show, Hope began the practice of working very closely with his writer, Wilkie Mahoney. Several nights a week the two would confer on the material planned for the upcoming show. The monologue had a short air-time span when broadcast. The topical nature of the gags and Hope's machine-gun rate of delivery required mountains of fresh material each week.

Once a decision on a subject was reached, the jokes had to be created to fit the topic. This involved long hours of hard work. Later, the material would be edited down to what both men agreed to be its funniest and freshest ten minutes.

Finally, in 1938, after years of living on the brink, Hope busted into the big time. Based on his success, both critical and popular, on "Your Hollywood Parade," Hope was signed by Pepsodent for his own show.

Typically for Hope, the big time was a long time coming. Fred Allen, Jack Benny and Bing Crosby all had cashed in years before.

By Hope's arrival they had become household names in America.

But he quickly made up for lost time. Despite the others' head start, he soon was challenging them in the "Hooper's" (ratings) and winning widespread critical acclaim.

The "Pepsodent Show" format was simple, no different from other shows of its ilk already being broadcast. Regular announcer Bill Goodwin introduced Bob, his guests and Skinnay Ennis and his band. Show regulars included Jerry Colonna, a kind of bizarre professor; Barbara Jo Allen in the role of Vera Vague; Blanche Stewart and Elvia Allman as Brenda and Cobina, parodies of famed society beauties of the day, Brenda Frazier and Cobina Wright, Jr.; and the vocal group, Six Hits and a Miss.

The singers included Pauline Byrries, Bill Sickler, Vincent Degen, Marnin Bailey, Jerry Preshaw, Howard Hudson and Mark McLean.

Judy Garland filled in quite nicely as featured female vocalist for more than a year. Others appearing were Frances Langford, Gloria Jean and Doris Day.

It was the execution of the show that made it different and unique. The tone for the show would be set by Hope's monologue, which was breezy, irreverent and spiced heavily with pointed allusions to current affairs. During the airing of one show, the comedian was clocked at seven jokes a minute.

The monologue was frequently controversial, causing ripples of concern in the sponsor's advertising agency that many times escalated into major flaps over image.

After the monologue came the skits and routines, which were characterized by zaniness not continuity, unlike the Benny or Allen shows, which used common everyday type characters and situations to launch laughs.

Preparation for the show was a grueling affair. The rehearsals were exhaustive. Determined to stay at the top, Hope hired a group of writers for the Pepsodent venture. Before very long, there were an even dozen.

At one time or another the Hope writing ranks included: Ted McKay, Mel Shavelson, Milt Josephsberg, Jack Rose, Norman Panama, Melvin Frank, Albert Schwartz, Norman Sullivan, Jack Douglas, Paul Laven, Dr. Samuel Kurtzman, Fred S. Fox, Hal Block and Larry Marks.

Recognizing that working with so many writers at one sitting would prove unwieldy, Hope devised a clever alternative. Each writer would be assigned to write an entire script each week. The subject would be the same for all. Foreign cars, for example.

At the script conference, each writer would read his effort aloud. Hope would record the response to each joke. The best would go into the master show script.

In addition to this novel approach to the creative aspects of comedy, Hope devised another technique to insure the success of his show.

The writers had to submit a ninety-minute script for the thirty-minute show. Once the ninety-minute rehearsal version was hammered out, two days of rehearsals followed. Then Hope and the cast would perform the ninety-minute version before a live audience and it would be recorded.

Hope and his staff then would select the best segments for the Tuesday night show.

This meticulous attention to detail and the pursuit of excellence was amply rewarded. In 1939, the Critics Poll of *Radio Daily* awarded Hope fourth ranking among radio's comedians. The poll:

Jack Benny	488
Fred Allen	376
Edgar Bergen	331
Bob Hope	321

The next year (1940), although the "Pepsodent Show" was voted second to Jack Benny's "Jello Show," 673 to 459, Bob Hope edged out Benny by 74 votes and became the top comedian in the country. The rise was meteoric, but, considering the backbreaking dedication, the acclaim was not astonishing.

Hope's comedy and its impact are difficult to re-create, because so much of it depended on an awareness of current affairs. However, the following excerpt from his March 12, 1940 show has fewer jokes of that nature than usual.

How do you do, ladies and gentlemen. This is Bob Hope advising you to use Pepsodent while your teeth are still underpups, and they won't grow up to be "Golden Boys." I'm a little tired tonight. I'm building a new house in North Hollywood, and I want to tell you that's hard work. I think I'll have to hire a carpenter to help me. It's one of those California all-weather houses ... you know ... six rooms, a big sun porch ... and a direct wire to the Coast Guard! I decided to build a permanent home now that I'm doing pretty well in pictures. Of course, it's the only house on the block with wheels on it! ... But I'm really putting up a nice house. The other day when the lumber came in ... the termites were standing around smacking their lips and applauding!

You'll like the inside of the house. It's really got a beautiful bathroom ... when you want cold water, all you have to do is dig ... when you want hot water ... you just go deeper! The other day I turned on the faucet, and a Major Bowes corroded unit came out! It's got three guest rooms ... the green room, the blue room, and the jade room. It's really all the same room ... we just change the lights for the first two and burn incense for the other! And I've got a new idea in the bedroom ... the walls just pull out from the bed. I have a Murphy bed and a Morris chair in my room, and the room is so small. The other morning Murphy woke up with an accent! One thing I don't like about the house is that is has a California Chamber of Commerce heating system. Everytime you turn it on it yells, "Traitor." The house should have been finished a long time ago ... But my architect drools, and every time he looks at the blueprints he inks in a couple of more rooms! The architect fixed it so that every time you go to the second floor you bump your head ... He calls it the "Stairway to the Stars"! But still it's going to be the show place of the town ... What other house in the neighborhood will have a neon fence? I got one of those new government loans on my house, and the government certainly protects its investments. The other day when it rained out here, Morgenthau called me up long distance to shut the windows! ... And here's Skinnay Ennis ...

This monologue illustrates the dual role Hope adopted in his comedy. The audience sometimes laughed with him as he zeroed in on famous figures as targets, such as Treasury Secretary Henry Morgenthau, Jr., well-known cabinet member in Roosevelt's administration.

But just as deftly, Hope set himself up as a target, as shown in the line, "I decided to build a permanent home ... " After the monologue the show continued with a song from Six Hits and a Miss.

Following a commercial, Hope added his own kind of praise for the product that was paying the bills. He said, "Yes, sir. Good old Pepsodent liquid dentifrice ... a drip in time saved mine." Other stars mocked their sponsor's products, so this approach was not new. But Hope's degree of irreverence was so intense, it made him far more daring than anyone else on radio.

Next on the program was a skit with Judy Garland and announcer Bill Goodwin. It illustrates the technique of using Hope as the target for laughter. Much like Jack Benny, who turned his alleged stinginess into a springboard for his comedy, Hope used his made-up character faults—his vanity, his lack of athletic prowess, his poor manners and the like—as material for the comedy routines.

Judy: Hello, Mr. Hope!

Hope: Hello, Judy. I've been looking for you. I want to thank you for that wonderful weekend we had at your house. I hope we didn't put your mother out too much.

Judy: Oh, no. Mother thought it was so nice that you could come on such short notice ... you gave her!

Goodwin: Gee, Judy, thanks for inviting me over, too.

Judy: You're welcome, Mr. Goodwin. It was nice of you to help my mother cook the dinner.

Hope: Goodwin helped your mother cook the dinner? Oh, *that's* what it was!

Goodwin: That's what *what* was?

Hope: Oh, nothing. But that was the first chicken I ever ate with irium gravy! [Irium was the additive in Pepsodent toothpaste.] ... But, Judy, I enjoyed everything so much I'm going to send your mother a nice autographed picture of myself.

Judy: Honest, Mr. Hope?

Hope: Why, sure.

Judy: Free?

Hope: Why, of course. I gave your father an autograph for nothing, didn't I?

Judy: Yes, and that reminds me. Daddy wants his pencil back.

Hope: I guess your mother thought we were pretty hungry the way we tore into that food we had for supper.

Judy: Oh, no. She was born and raised on a farm, she's used to those noises ... But she did say that was the first time she ever saw anyone get sparks out of a knife and fork!

Hope: Gosh, everything was marvelous ... You know, it was all new to me, having breakfast in bed.

Judy: By the way, Mr. Hope, my servant told me to tell you ... when you eat in bed you should *sit up*.

Hope: I *thought* something was wrong. After I ate those soft-boiled eggs, *I looked like "Golden Boy."*

Judy; Our home isn't very big. Did you mind sleeping over the garage?*Hope*: Oh, not at all. I had a beautiful *carbon monoxide* dream.

Judy: I guess Skinnay Ennis spent a restless night, too. You know, Mr. Hope, Skinnay walks in his sleep.

Hope: Does he?

Hope and Jane Russell, his co-star in Paleface and Son of Paleface, doing a routine for his radio show

A famous duo in radio and television

Judy: Yes. I could hear him all night long banging against the walls of his iron lung.

Hope: Well, I slept all right, except I heard a peculiar noise during the night, sort of metallic clinking.

Judy: Oh, that! That was only daddy downstairs counting the silverware.

Hope: By the way it was the finest mattress I ever slept on the floor next to.

Judy: I meant to ask you before, Mr. Hope. Why did you stay in your room all Sunday afternoon?

Hope: Well, after all, Judy, it takes *me* a little time to *understand* the funny papers.

Judy: Was it exciting?

Hope: Exciting! I'll say it was ... Dick Tracy almost caught *himself!*

Judy: Mr. Hope, you didn't get mad when those kids from across the street lighted a fire under you when you were sitting on the barbecue pit, did you?

Hope: No, I was just surprised. I thought someone had stolen my secret formula for the Hope Hotfoot.

Judy: You were nice about everything. My mother wants to thank you for mowing the lawn, and my brother wants to thank you, too.

Hope: Your brother wants to thank me for mowing the lawn?

Judy: Not exactly. He was lying on it at the time ... and he has *always wanted one of those college boy haircuts!*

Hope: Well, I'm glad I did *something* right. I didn't look so good when we were out on the tennis courts. I thought I was a good tennis player, but I was really outclassed.

Judy: Well, don't you feel bad about it, Mr. Hope. Miss Robson is awfully fast on her feet.

Hope: Oh, I felt better after the beating she gave George Arliss.

Judy: I liked your tennis outfit. But weren't those shorts you wore kind of long?

Hope: Judy, those weren't shorts. They were my white flannel pants from high school graduation.

Judy: Well, they were up above your knees. Mr. Hope, don't you think it would be better if you just wore your socks without the garters?

Hope: I'll try that. Next time I'll just hook them over my kneecaps.

Judy: That was some sign you hung out in the street before the match.

Hope: I designed it myself, Judy—just a simple White banner with two-foot red letters. Did you like the wording?

Judy: Oh, yes ... "Tennis game now on ... starring Bob Hope."

Hope: I thought I did very well in the first two games.

Judy: You did. I even liked you when they put the net up! Say, why did Mr. Ennis keep holding his tennis racket up to his face?

Hope: Judy, Skinnay had that racket built special. It's got smelling salts in the handle. I thought I was really good in my match with Mickey Rooney.

Judy: That was exciting.

Hope: I smashed the ball as hard as I could. Mickey smashed it right back. Boy, can he hit! He drove it so hard, when it stopped bouncing, the ball said, "Listen, fellers, can't we settle this thing some other way?"

Judy: We did have a good time, didn't we? But I'm so sorry the swimming pool didn't have any water in it.

Hope: Yes. It was nice of Mickey Rooney *not* to tell me!

Judy: Did you get hurt?

Hope: Of course not. It was all in fun. I can pick up a new shoulder blade anyplace.

It is quite easy to see that the comedy on Hope's show was basically one-dimensional with ridicule the major objective. The object of the ridicule might be Hope or Ennis or anyone. But there was no attempt at characterization, the focal point of the "Jack Benny Show." Nor were topics ever explored in depth as they were on the "Fred Allen Show." The plot for the skits was skimpy and the laughs were dependent entirely upon the one-liners.

Furthermore, the audience was always aware that the wisecracks were always meant in jest. Hope never intended his comedy to be anything more than what it was—a vehicle for laughs. His comedy was not meant to be social satire or to be used for didactic purposes.

Colonna illustrated this approach to comedy, as in this routine:

(*The telephone rings and Hope picks it up*)

Colonna: Hope hello. Colonna is this.

Hope: Colonna, why are you talking backwards.

Colonna: Put the nickel in upside down.

Hope: That wouldn't have anything to do with it, Colonna.

Colonna: Okay.

(*Sound: Animal bellowing and snorting*)

Hope: What's that Colonna?

Colonna: I'm pulling the buffalo out by his tail.
Hope: That's impossible.
Colonna: I don't ask questions. I just have fun.

Colonna and Barbara Jo Allen (the Vera Vague character) were unique to Hope's offering, for they were the only performers to remain on the show over an extended period. Unlike other radio comedians, Hope discovered that his type of show didn't require a large supporting cast on a regular basis.

Vera Vague, who belied her name, provided the counterthrust to Hope's simulated pompousness and vanity. As played by Barbara Jo Allen, she was quick-witted and clear-thinking.

In one routine Hope pointed to a group of Marines in the audience and observed that the Marines always attacked an enemy from all sides, "squeezing and squeezing." Hearing this, Vera stuck out her tongue in the direction of the men.

Ordered by Hope to stop, she replied, "It seemed like a good idea at the time."

Hope: I suppose at one time you seemed like a good idea.
Vera: You say such clever things, Mr. Hope. Really, I wish I had your head. It'd look so nice stuffed over the mantlepiece ... These Marines are so wonderful ... I wish my boy friend Waldo had joined up with them.
Hope: What branch is Waldo in now?
Vera: Usually the one overlooking Hedy Lamarr's window!

With wide, round and rolling eyes and a lush mustache, Jerry Colonna occupied a unique place on the Hope show. He sounded every bit as insane as he looked. His portrayal of the character named Yehudi became a part of radio folklore.

A mythical "search" for Yehudi provided material for many shows. The so-called search climaxed with the appearance of Basil Rathbone and Nigel Bruce, famous for their roles as supersleuth Sherlock Holmes and Doctor Watson, his addle-brained assistant.

Colonna was a leading character in Hope's most infamous and controversial radio broadcast.

Playing the part of Santa Claus, Colonna was killed by Hope; in the script, that is. The show had no sooner left the air when the network was deluged with telephone calls of protest from outraged listeners. Telegrams and letters quickly followed from shocked parents who failed to see the humor in the foul episode.

The level of reaction was so intense against the Santa caper that for a brief time the Pepsodent people feared they would be forced to cancel the show.

But the quick-to-forget public quickly forgot, and the brash Hope continued to short-circuit the radio waves with outrageous comedy. His belief that such a routine would be well received no doubt stemmed from his growing success at using skits, gags and routines other radio comedians shied away from.

His scripts frequently skirted the edge of lewdness, according to the prevailing standards of the day, showing him to be, on occasion, the master of the double-entendre. For example:

Hope: Some park.
Girl: Some park.
Hope: Some grass.
Girl: Some grass.
Hope: Some dew.
Girl: I don't.

Hope sought to add another dimension to his comedy by pulling an old trick that had proved very successful in radio over the years. He arranged a feud with singer Bing Crosby.

The feud gambit first was heard over the air in 1927. The so-called adversaries then were Nils T. Granlund and Harry Richman. Later, the same bit was used by Ben Bernie and Walter Winchell in that pair's celebrated "dispute."

Two of radio's greatest traditional comedians, Jack Benny and Fred Allen, transformed their feigned dislike for one another into a topic of daily conversation across America, and into a surefire rating grabber the night each performer's program was to be aired.

Hope's feud with Crosby was in the same tradition. Crosby seemed to bring out the best in Hope. The exchanges between the two rank among the funniest routines Hope ever performed. Most were heard on radio, but the feud was intensified in film, fueled by their relationship in the *Road* movies.

The Hope-Crosby feud was based strictly on Hope's open envy of Crosby's wealth, leading-man status and singing ability. Frequently, Hope would retort to Crosby's needling by making sly reference to the singer's age and his need to wear a hairpiece. Another target for Hope's scorn was Crosby's ears, which were large and kind of floppy.

In this brief excerpt from one of Hope's radio shows, it is easy to see that both men approached the task of feeding the feud with energy, enthusiasm and genuine enjoyment:

Crosby: Sorry I'm late, Bob. I had trouble finding a place to park.
Hope: What do you mean? The stable's right outside.
Crosby: Is that what that was? I thought it was your dressing room. It was—last time I was on your show.
Hope: That was last time. They moved me out to the garage. It was the least they could do.
Crosby: How do you mean that?
Hope: I asked for a raise.
Crosby: That takes nerve. You haven't been able to get a raise out of your audience in years.
Hope: Tell me, Bing. With so much hot air and those ears, why don't you take off?
Crosby: The downdraft from your nose prevents it.
Hope: Why do we fight? You know I really like you.
Crosby: Only when you've been on Army bases too long.

On other occasions the feud was a rapid-fire exchange of epithets.

Crosby: As I live, ski snoot.
Hope: Mattress hip.
Crosby: Shovel head.
Hope: Blubber.
Crosby: Scoop nose.
Hope: Lard.
Crosby: Yes, Dad.

The last line showed Crosby, dubbed the crooner by music critics and the groaner by Hope, striking back handily.

Much like the movie version of the feud, the Hope-Crosby tilt hit the road in the early forties on radio too. Hope began entertaining servicemen and broadcasting his show from military bases and posts around the country. He started the custom in 1941 as a part of the war effort. He continued to do his Pepsodent broadcast from military bases until June, 1948.

Many of Hope's funniest monologues were inspired by the military life. His penchant for incorporating local references into his material brought him instant rapport with his servicemen audiences and the general listening public, as well.

The following monologue was broadcast in March, 1943.

How do you do, ladies and gentlemen, this is Bob "Broadcasting

Frances Langford and Bob don't appreciate Jerry Colonna's trombone playing

from the Naval Air Station at Los Alamitos" Hope, telling you naval aviators that whether you're just an ordinary student or at the head of your class ... be sure to use Pepsodent and your teeth will never be washed out in a glass ... Well, here I am at Los Alamitos, a nice quiet little town ... I wouldn't say Los Alamitos is small ... but it looks like something Henry J. Kaiser built during his lunch hour ... Los Alamitos is so small it's the only place in America where the draft board had to draft the draft board ... I got a wonderful reception when I arrived here. Every naval flier in the place made a rush for me as I walked in ... wearing a heavy veil and a low-cut evening gown ... the naval cadets seldom see girls here ... in fact, this is one of the few places where your copy of *Esquire* comes with an interpreter ... but I'm happy to be among you men of the Navy. You know, my family goes back to John Paul Jones ... in fact, they went back to John Paul Jones so often the bottle was empty before I got there ... but you all know Thursday's April Fool's Day and the youngsters are beginning to play pranks already ... I reached down for a wallet in the middle of the street in Los Alamitos and some kid with a string pulled it away ... he didn't fool me long though ... and it was only a short bus trip back from San Diego ... just to see if the government's got a sense of humor, my brother sent back his income tax return signed April fool ... they've got a sense of humor ... my brother is now at Leavenworth till next April, the fool ... this year in Hollywood, I saw a crowd of civilians going crazy ... they were gathered outside of the post office and the President of the ration board was leaning out of the window with a T-bone steak on a yo-yo ... and you know how the kids in the neighborhood always put a brick under an old derby so when you kick it you'll break your toes? ... I'm too smart to be fooled by that old derby gag, so when I stepped outside my house yesterday and saw one I just heaved a rock at it ... as soon as I get my house built again I'm gonna find out where those kids got that land mine ... but isn't this a beautiful auditorium? We're thrilled to be the first show to come out of this recreation hall which was just built ... well, it wasn't exactly built ... they just turned on the garden hose and waited for a sandstorm ... in fact, the building is so new, the paint still smells ... they say "no" but I still insist it's the paint ... but everything is clean and fresh ... I've been giving my house a little spring cleaning this week ... I wanted to clean out my Frigidaire, but my relatives beat me to it ... what a cleaning job I did ... my doorbell rang and I answered it in my apron and old dust cap ... some woman looked me over and shoved a paper in my hand. I thought she wanted my autograph, so I signed it ... how do you resign from the Wacs?

90

Hope's radio show continued to be popular with listeners through-out the forties. However, the critics began to desert him after the war ended. His 1947 season premiere was greeted harshly by the taste-makers.

The *Variety* reviewer wrote:

> Here's the epitome of radio's "sad saga of sameness." Appar-ently it's just too much to expect that Hope would veer an inch from his timetested routine. His answer, it goes without saying, is: Why get out of the rut as long as there's pay dirt in it? And top pay dirt at that! By Hooper's count, too, Hope seems to be justified. His routine is apparently one of the things we fought the war for, like Ma's apple pie. Question simply is: Who's going to outlive the other, Hope or the listening public?
>
> What happened on Hope's curtain raiser of his 10th season last week was just more of the same, and too much of it. The old gagmaster and his insult-for-insult sparring mates, Colonna and Miss Vague, let go the usual snappers about Hope's nose, his writers, the sponsor, Eagle Rock and Santa Monica, etc. Van Heflin, who sleuthed as "Philip Marlow" during Hope's summer layoff, kept coming into the act with a routine about still having that last culprit to catch. Georgia Gibbs, first guest vocalist on the show, piped a nicely contrived version of "Feudin' and Fightin'." The studio audience, performing as usual, knocked itself out clapping. Hodgepodgey as the act was, it clicked for laughs at the accustomed pace until the last five minutes, which turned into a fuddled mess of lost lines, garbled action and wild guffawing, though perplexing to the listener.

It was a very rude welcome, but Hope weathered the season intact. However, the cold critical reception started Hope wondering whether the listeners felt the same.

During the next year, Hope decided to clean house. Jerry Colonna and Barbara Jo Allen (Vera Vague) were dropped. Looking for a fresher image and approach, Hope added top female singers like Doris Day as featured attractions. These guests appeared in the skits in addition to doing their song spots.

Hope opened his eleventh radio season with a new sponsor too. Soap plugs replaced toothpaste plugs—Lever Brothers for Pepsodent. But the old zing was missing. The caliber of the show continued to plummet. Not unexpectedly the ratings followed suit.

In January of 1949, the ratings were 23.8; by 1951, 12.7; and in 1953 a dismal 5.4. In fairness to Hope, there was a perfectly simple reason why he was losing his radio listeners. They had bought television sets.

Neither he himself nor the advertising business was willing to count Hope out of radio. In 1953 he signed the biggest single season deal in radio history, a $2 million contract with General Foods for six shows a week. There was a surprising twist. Hope was to leave America's living rooms to entertain in its kitchens—the shows were to be aired during the day.

His new contract called for a fifteen-minute show broadcast at 9:30 A.M. Monday through Friday, and a thirty-minute weekly evening variety show. Everyone loved the arrangement. The sponsor, the listeners and, yes, the critics. *Variety* welcomed Hope's daytime debut this way:

> This is the new Bob Hope daytime show and it may well set the pattern for a complete reshuffle in network radio programming, in that a number of other name personalities may follow Hope into the after-breakfast hours if he can draw a rating. On his initialer Monday, in fact, a group of such stars (on hand to congratulate Hope on his new venture) might have been indulging in a little kidding-on-the-square as they cracked about the dough Hope is pulling in. Hope's show is costing Jell-O $2,000,000 ...
>
> That Hope will draw a hefty daytime rating is virtually a certainty. The show is obviously taped at a more respectable hour than its airtime (which would make it 6:30 a.m. on the Coast) and, as a result, he and his announcer, Bill Goodwin, plus their gueststars, are in top form ... the Tuesday stanza gave indication that the show is Hope at his oldtime radio best—and that's good.

Although Hope's experiment with daytime radio was successful and his show lasted for five years, he eventually decided to stop bucking the tide. Radio listeners wanted music and talk shows. Radio comedy had lost its appeal.

FILMS AND FILMOGRAPHY

As with his vaudeville, Broadway and radio careers, Hope's film career was not characterized by instant stardom. It was typically slow in the beginning.

Through the intervention of Al Boasberg, his writer during the vaudeville days, Hope was given a screen test in 1930 for Pathé Studios. Bill Perlberg (of the later famous producer-director team of Perlberg-Seaton) was a Hollywood agent at the time. He had arranged the test at the urging of Boasberg, an old friend.

The test consisted of Hope doing a "single" followed by his vaudeville act with his partner, Louise Troxell.

Although Hope remembers that the response of the studio crew was enthusiastic, the test itself was a dismal failure. Hope later recalled: "I'd never seen anything so awful. I looked like a cross between a mongoose and a turtle. I couldn't wait to get out."

His next fling with the movies occurred on a decidedly lesser scale. Even the locale of the encounter lacked the glamour and the magic of Hollywood. The studio was in Astoria, a section of Queens in New York City.

In 1934, while appearing in *Roberta* on Broadway, Hope was signed by Educational Pictures to appear in one film short subject with the option for five others if all went well. The first short was an educational musical comedy entitled *Going Spanish*.

The filming in the Astoria studio went smoothly. The short was written by William Watson and Art Jarrett and produced and directed by Al Christie. Hope's co-star was Leah Ray.

However, Hope was not pleased with his performance, although he felt that Miss Ray had fared very well. His dissatisfaction led to Hope's business arrangement with Educational Pictures being briefer than either party had anticipated.

It happened that a glum and glib Hope went to see himself at a

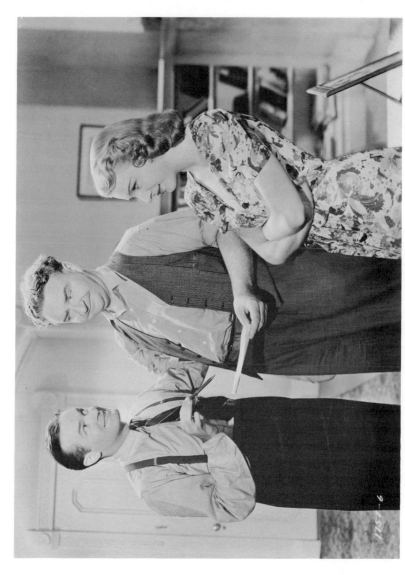

After the success of the song, Hope and Shirley Ross were reteamed in a film titled Thanks for the Memory

movie house in Manhattan on the same day as powerful columnist Walter Winchell. They bumped into one another while leaving, and Winchell asked Hope for his reaction.

Winchell reported Hope's candid reply in his column the next day. "When Bob Hope saw his picture at the Rialto, he said, 'When they catch John Dillinger, the current public enemy number one, they're going to make him sit through it twice.'"

Hope's crack was good copy, but Educational Pictures somehow failed to see the humor. They immediately dropped his option.

However, within a short time Warner Brothers signed the aspiring motion picture star for a series of shorts and trailers. His first venture was entitled, *Paree, Paree*, directed by Ray Mack and co-starring Dorothy Stone, Charles Collins, Billie Leonard and Lorraine Collier.

After *Paree, Paree* in 1934, Hope made six more shorts. *The Old Gray Mayor*, *Watch the Birdie* and *Double Exposure*, were filmed in 1935, followed in 1936 by *Calling All Tars* and *Shop Talk*. All were directed by Lloyd French.

Hope's final short film during this period was called *Don't Hook Now*. It was made in 1938 and in it Hope played himself at a golf tournament. The short became an important film industry footnote because it marked the first time Hope and Bing Crosby appeared together in a motion picture.

Hope's debut in a full-length movie came in *The Big Broadcast of 1938*. Two factors played major roles in the decision to award Hope a featured part in the film—availability and luck. Jack Benny, who had been slated for the part, was unable to do it. Mitchell Leisen, the director, and Harlan Thompson remembered Hope from one of his Broadway shows and decided he'd make an ideal replacement for the busy Benny. When they called to make Hope the offer, he didn't refuse. The Hopes moved to California.

The film was Hollywood's rendition of a musical revue. The trade name for this type of movie was "clambake," meaning just about everything was in it.

And just about everybody, too. Paramount contract-players between jobs were written into the script. They included W. C. Fields, Martha Raye, Shirley Ross, Lynn Overman and Ben Blue, to name a few. The film also was a reunion for Hope with his former radio comedy sidekick, Honey Chile Wilder, and with singer Dorothy Lamour. Both ladies had known Hope in New York.

Hope played Buzz Fielding, the master of ceremonies. Shirley

A poster for his 1940 film, The Ghostbreakers

Lamour, Crosby, Hope and Dona Drake in a scene from The Road to Morocco (1942)

Ross portrayed his film wife. In the script, their stormy marriage has ended in divorce, after which they meet by chance on a transatlantic liner. A few friendly drinks are followed by a reconciliation scene in song.

The couple review their marital history by singing a duet entitled, "Thanks for the Memory." The film and Hope's part in it would have been quickly forgotten had it not been for a rave review by columnist Damon Runyon—of the song, not the film.

Runyon saw a preview, and wrote a glowing review. It said simply, "What a delivery, what a song, what an audience reception." The review was Hope's first unqualified critical success since he had ventured west. He never forgot what it meant to him.

He didn't forget the song either. He made it his signature. Millions of people all over the world probably don't know the words, but more than likely they can hum the first few bars.

Runyon's item was invaluable publicity, but it made little impression on the Paramount front office, which tended to view a movie actor's future strictly in terms of the box-office present.

Thus, Hope's next part was a very minor role in a "B" movie, *College Swing*, which was being produced by Lewis Gensler. The main reason Hope was slated for such a small part was that his solid vaudeville and Broadway credits meant little in Hollywood. And it should be remembered here that Hope had yet to make his splash in radio.

Hope realized his part would have to be meatier if he was to catch on with the public, so he appealed directly to Gensler. Fortunately, the producer had fond recollections of Hope as a Broadway pro. Both had been associated with the production of *Ballyhoo of 1932*.

Hope's role was enlarged, but in retrospect it was largely the impact of Runyon's timely comment and Hope's pluck that enabled him to survive professionally the career impact of his next four pictures.

Give Me a Sailor (1938), *Thanks for the Memory* (1938), *Never Say Die* (1939) and *Some Like It Hot* (1939) were mediocre, easily forgotten and gross misuses of his considerable comic talent.

In his fifth Paramount film, *The Cat and the Canary*, Hope was finally cast in a role tailored to his talent. The movie was based on the mystery-melodrama play by John Willard. For the screen version, screenwriters Walter De Leon and Lynn Starling rewrote it into a farce in hopes of producing laughs instead of suspense.

The plot revolves around Wally Hampton, a mystery story buff

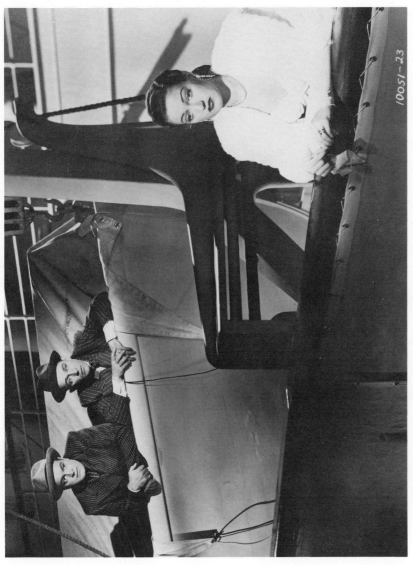

Bob and Bing looking on as Dorothy Lamour contemplates suicide in The Road to Rio (1948)

As usual, Bing and Bob are wrestling for Dottie's "hand"; Road to Rio (1948)

played by Hope, who unwittingly finds himself in the midst of a real-life thriller. A young heiress, played by Paulette Goddard, is justifiably frightened about her life being in danger, but she can't convince anyone of the threat except Hope. He believes in her and sets out to help her.

In the process Hope and Goddard spoofed every aspect of the traditional mystery-melodrama. They won critical acclaim and box-office success for their efforts.

"Streamlined, screamlined, played to the hilt for comedy, the new version is more harebrained than hairraising," wrote Frank Nugent in the *New York Times*.

Howard Barnes in the *Herald Tribune* singled out Hope: "Mr. Hope is a pillar of strength in holding the film to its particular mood of satirical melodrama."

Though the immediate success of the film and the good notices were critically important to Hope's film career in 1939, *The Cat and the Canary*'s long-range significance to him was not immediately recognized. In Wally Hampton Hope had found the skeleton of the screen character around which he would mold his future screen image. In many instances, Wally Hampton was the prototype for all of Hope's successful screen characterizations. The reluctant heroism of Hampton, and his penchant for quips when confronted by perilous situations, eventually became Hope's film trademarks.

Asked, "Don't big empty houses scare you?" he replies, "Not me. I used to be in vaudeville." Or, "I always joke when I'm scared, I kid myself that I'm brave."

Hope, unveiled his celebrated chicken heart as Wally Hampton saying: "Even my goosepimples get goose pimples."

He also displayed his affection for the topical quip by answering the question, "Do you believe in reincarnation—you know, that dead people always come back?" with the rejoinder, "You mean like the Republicans?"

A third side of his future screen personality—the lady killer—is shown in its embryonic stage by the Hampton comment, "My mother brought me up never to be caught twice in the same lady's bedroom."

The success of *The Cat and the Canary* prompted Paramount to reunite Hope with Goddard in the 1940 film, *The Ghostbreakers*. A well-worn property, the film was a remake of the 1922 version starring Wallace Reid, which was a remake of the 1915 version with H. B. Warner. (Paramount remade it again in 1953 as *Scared Stiff*,

Bing Crosby and Bob Hope as circus performers on the lam in Road to Rio *(1948)*

with Dean Martin and Jerry Lewis, in which Hope appeared as an unbilled walk-on.)

Ghostbreakers was patterned after its predecessor in that the story line was incidental to the gags. A haunted castle in Cuba served as a device to bring off all the sinister and spooky happenings that are predictably inspired by such an edifice. It was all rather obvious. But neither the critics nor the audiences seemed to mind the lack of concern with such essentials as plot, credibility, originality and so on.

An enthusiastic Bosley Crowther wrote in part: "It worked out very nicely in 'The Cat and the Canary' last year, and it is working quite as nicely and even more amusingly, in fact—in 'The Ghostbreakers!' "

Prior to his role in *Ghostbreakers* Hope had co-starred in *Road to Singapore* with Bing Crosby and Dorothy Lamour. Considering the trio's subsequent success in the *Road* pictures, it is fascinating to note the role luck played in their selection. Paramount choose Hope and Crosby for expediency. George Burns and Gracie Allen were slated to be the original leads when a scheduling conflict arose. Paramount then sought Fred MacMurray and Jack Oakie. They too had other commitments.

By this time Hope had become accustomed to being second choice. He had won the big part in the Broadway play, *Red, Hot and Blue*, only after William Gaxton had turned it down. His role in *The Big Broadcast of 1938* originally had been offered to Jack Benny.

The Road to Singapore was first named *The Road to Mandalay*, but executives decided to retitle it because Mandalay didn't sound treacherous enough. This decision didn't help the film's plot, which bordered on the innocuous.

Briefly, a son of a rich shipping tycoon (Crosby) and his knockaround buddy (Hope) meet a sarong (Lamour). Both men fall in love with her. In 1940, the raven-haired Lamour was easily an eye and armful. Her charms were amply displayed to their best advantage in the clinging native sarong. So much for the sex interest.

Native lady Lamour really digs Crosby's unassuming rich boy act, but she feels unworthy of him, so she initially clings in Hope's direction. Her sense of unworthiness is reinforced in an encounter with Crosby's tycoon Dad, who has his errant son's fiancée in tow. So much for the chase scene.

Before the finale true love triumphs. Hope realizes he's actually just a good friend to Lamour. He steps aside, enabling his

Hope and Crosby "on the road to Rio" (1948)

Attempting to flee from their assailants while "on the road," Hope and Crosby invariably don a disguise. In this scene from Road to Rio (1948) the boys portray South American dancers

competition (Crosby) to win the sarong forever, or at least until the next *Road* picture.

The skimpy story line is augmented by a series of madcap adventures involving Hope and Crosby. The pair use the scrapes as a backdrop for their gags, quips and asides to the audience. The slaphappy attitude adopted by the cavorting duo during the impromptu escapades adds to the laughs.

Much of the appeal of the picture lies in the ambivalent comradery of Hope and Crosby. Ostensibly buddies, the pair actually engage in fierce rivalry over money, sex and personal vanity. While competing for Lamour's affections, neither has any compunction about publicly disclosing the other's penchant for philandering. Hope alludes to Crosby's age with references to senility while Crosby dismisses Hope with the disclaiming, "Junior."

The characterizations for all future *Road* movies are derived from *Singapore*. Hope is an overanxious, overeager, aggressive, bumbling lover who talks a good story to bolster his own false confidence. Crosby is the suave, quietly cool type who will inevitably win the girl without seeming to try.

They share some traits and are not complete opposites. Both men exhibit an unwillingness to settle down, an oft-repeated aversion to matrimony but an insatiable appetite for what leads up to it and a distinct distaste for physical violence. They also demonstrate an ability to wisecrack out of tight spots using old vaudeville routines. The famous patty-cake bit makes its debut in *Singapore*.

The film's glaring flaw is its unevenness. The movie falters in many of the scenes in which Hope and Crosby appear with Lamour because of their serious tone. When Crosby loses her to Hope, the scene is too sentimental. Instead of being flip, Crosby is philosophical when he tells Lamour: "He'll cost you a lot of trouble and never make a penny, but he'll hand you a million laughs."

Despite its uneven quality, *The Road to Singapore* received generally favorable reviews. Frank S. Nugent of the *New York Times* observed, "The comedy is going along swimmingly until boys meet sarong." More importantly, the film was a hit at the box office.

Road to Zanzibar, the next *Road* outing, was made in 1941. It was a follow up to *Singapore*, to cash in on the prior film's success. The eventual extent of the *Road* series was not contemplated at this time. But the potential for the series was obvious, for as Don Hartman, one of the writers on *Road to Singapore*, foresaw: "You take a piece of used chewing gum and flip it at a map. Wherever it sticks you can

Bing and Bob in one of their customary predicaments in Road to Bali (1953)

lay a Road picture, so long as the people there are jokers who cook and eat strangers. If they're nasty and menacing, it'll be a good Road picture. The key to the thing is menace offsetting the humor."

The Road to Zanzibar was originally a serious and dramatic tale about two men lost in the tangled jungles of Madagascar. It was written by Sy Bartlett, who called it *Find Colonel Fawcett*. It was rejected in its original form since its story line had such a strong resemblance to the just released *Stanley and Livingston*. Frank Butler and Don Hartman, the screenwriters on *Singapore*, rewrote the script as a comedy and changed the locale to Zanzibar.

Zanzibar is far better than *Singapore*. The entire film is played for laughs, with none of the tentative seriousness that dogged its predecessor. Lamour's role is deemphasized and the predictable romantic entanglements are incorporated into the comic treatment.

The accent on comedy is reinforced by the billing. Lamour, who received second billing in *Singapore*, is third to Crosby and Hope respectively in *Zanzibar*. The film successfully burlesqued Hollywood's musical jungle pictures. The script is far better than *Singapore*'s, and Hope and Crosby enliven the proceedings with frequent ad libs as they did so well in *Singapore*.

Reminiscing about this aspect of the *Road* pictures, Crosby remembered:

Our first "Road" picture baffled its director, Victor Schertzenger. Victor was a nice fellow and he'd directed some fine pictures, but he'd had little experience with low comedy. He was an experienced musician, and although he knew nothing about hokum, Paramount signed him to direct the first "Road" picture because of his musical background. He was a quiet fellow, used to directing his pictures in a leisurely fashion. His awakening was rude. For a couple of days, when Hope and I tore freewheeling into a scene, ad libbing and violating all the accepted rules of movie making, Schertzenger stole bewildered looks at his script, then leafed rapidly through it, searching for the lines we were saying.

When he couldn't find them he'd be ready to flag us down and say reprovingly, "Perhaps we'd better do it the way it's written gentlemen," but then he'd notice that the crew was laughing at our antics. He was smart enough to see that if we evoked that kind of merriment from a hard boiled gang who'd seen so many pictures they were blase about them, it might be good to let us do it our way.

So we had more trouble from our writers than our director ... They didn't like the way we kicked their prose around, and it didn't help that when they visited our set we ad libbed in spades. When

Bing, Bob and Dottie in a production number from Bali (1953)

Bing, Bob and Dottie in a scene from Bali (1953)

Hope called out to Hartman [the same Don Hartman], "If you recognize anything of yours, yell, bingo." Don left the set in a huff to register a beef with the production department.

We were curious as to what the front office thought of our antics, so when the eleven o'clock rushes were run off, Hope and I sneaked into the projection room. All the studio executives were in there, the door was ajar, and we could hear those inside guffawing. They even roared when Hope stopped the action and talked directly to the audience, a most unorthodox procedure. So we knew we were in.

Zanzibar was a critical smash. Howard Barnes of the *New York Herald Tribune* led the parade with: "Road to Zanzibar is mostly nonsense but it is nonsense of the most delightful sort." The following year *The Road to Morocco* was filmed, which in retrospect emerged as one of the best of the series. From the onset of the credits, during which Hope and Crosby perched on camels singing the title song, to its zany climax, *Morocco* was a joyous frolic.

The film's plot is funnier than previous *Road* pix. Crosby and Hope are broke, a fairly typical situation. But then Crosby sells Hope into slavery to remedy his situation. Later, Crosby dreams about Hope's plight. Hope's Aunt Lucy, played by Hope, appears in Crosby's dream to rebuke him for abandoning her nephew to barbarians. Duly chastised and appropriately contrite, Crosby decides to launch a search and rescue mission.

But circumstances have been kind to captive Hope in the interim. His captor is Dorothy Lamour, a pagan princess. Hope has managed to endear himself to Dorothy and her bevy of beautiful maids in waiting to such a great degree that he has become the palace favorite.

Hope is blissfully unaware that he actually is being set up to fulfill a prophecy. Lamour is bethrothed to desert prince Anthony Quinn, a lusty and glamorous man. But a fortune-teller has predicted that Lamour's first marriage is doomed to be short and dismal while her second is a sure bet to be long and glorious.

Thus, Lamour has developed a great affection for Hope, seeing in him unlimited victim potential. But then fate in the person of Crosby steps in and all plans go awry. Forgetting Quinn, Lamour promptly falls in love with the rescue-minded Crosby, who is truly astonished by his abandoned pal's incredible luck. With Lamour all over Crosby, Hope ties up with handmaiden Dona Drake. The climax of the film is a dramatic escape by the lovestruck quartet from the wrath of a jilted Quinn.

111

Dottie, Bob and Bing encounter some unexpected company in Road to Bali (1953)

Morocco's zany plot provided Hope with several opportunities to embellish his screen character. In one of the film's funniest scenes, Hope finds himself the unexpected object of lavish attention from Lamour. Lolling on a mountain of silk and velvet cushions, Hope is shown brushing away a spicy delicacy with an air of bored lordliness.

Next, he interrupts his water-pipe smoking to bare his teeth, for the moment fully savoring his lush life in bondage. The scene closes when he licks a lollipop with sensual gusto, as if to say, if this is being a sucker, then I love it.

The aura of the pagan palace serves as a springboard for some of Hope's better lines. Bondage has proven so beautiful that at one point he announces: "I'm going to be a pasha, with the accent on the pash." Later, as he is being tenderly caressed by a gorgeous harem mate, Hope sighs contentedly, commenting: "Mother told me there'd be moments like this." Reflecting on what he thinks is the key to his successful conquest of the princess, he remarks: "Sheiks have gone out of style. What the modern girl needs is a nice reliable wolf."

With the arrival of Crosby at the palace, the ensuing competition for Lamour's favors results in a bonanza of typical Hope-Crosby banter. After a passionate kiss, the curled toes of Hope's slippers straighten, prompting an envious Crosby to crack: "Now kiss him on the nose and see if you can straighten that out."

Hope retaliates later in a scene with Quinn, who threatens Crosby and calls him a moonfaced son of a one-eyed donkey. Hope advises Crosby: "I wouldn't let him call me that even if there *is* a resemblance."

Hope the coward is also shown in a restaurant scene when penniless he worries about what the owner may do when the meal ends and it's time to collect the bill. "Those guys have got knives; they might try to get the food back the hard way," he says.

Both Hope's and Crosby's ribald enthusiasm for sex becomes a source of laughter during the scene in which Hope feigns a disinterest in man's oldest diversion. Seeming to reject a slave girl's embraces, he explains offhandedly, "You gotta catch me in the mood for that sort of thing."

Crosby immediately holds Hope to account for the outrageous gaff by cracking, "You haven't been out of it for twenty years." Hope's retort refers to age. "You've got everything I've got and you've had it so much longer," he replies.

Hope enjoying the good life in the last Road—to Hong Kong (1962)

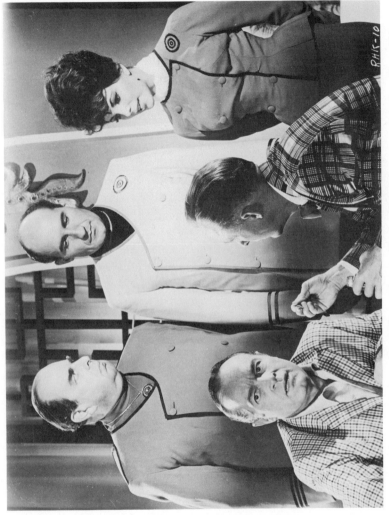

Bob, Bing and Joan Collins accosted by two menacing characters in Road to Hong Kong *(1962), the last of the series*

Topicality, another Hope comedy device, is utilized in a short scene in which Hope makes reference to a book entitled *How to Make Love: Six Lessons from Madame La Zonga.*

The second part of the book title is an allusion to a film of the same name which was being shown at the time *Morocco* was being made. The identical technique is also used in the dream sequence previously mentioned when Hope, playing his Aunt Lucy, appears to a sleeping Crosby. The scene ends when Hope tells Crosby, "I can't talk anymore. Here Comes Mr. Jordan," the last sentence being the title of another current film.

Morocco offers several musical interludes of the type that were standard fare in the *Road* movie formula. The title song is a spoof of the *Road* concept and its lyrics include the verse, "I'll lay you eight to five we meet Dorothy Lamour." Crosby croons a romantic ballad, "Moonlight Becomes You So," and Lamour upholds her end of the singing credits with a rendition of "Constantly."

The critical notices for *Morocco* varied. The lead camel in the film beat the critics to a review by pronouncing, "This is the screwiest picture I was ever in." Having obviously enjoyed the film as sheer and harmless nonsense, the *New York Times* man hailed it. "It is in short a lampoon of all pictures having to do with exotic romance, played by a couple of wise guys who can make a gag do everything but lay an egg," he explained.

A stuffier Howard Barnes of the *Herald Tribune* flatly denounced the movie as a Paramount contribution to decadence. "Paramount has been teetering on the edge of antic vulgarity in several Bing Crosby, Bob Hope, Dorothy Lamour road pictures. It takes a nose dive with the 'Road to Morocco,'" he declared angrily.

Barnes went on to predict that despite its alleged pandering to bad taste, the film would almost certainly be a huge hit. He was dead right. It was.

Barnes also forecast that *Morocco* would be the last of its kind, writing: "The fact remains that Road to Morocco represents the end of a dead street for this particular type of Hollywood nonsense." He was dead wrong. It wasn't.

Three years after *Morocco*, in 1945, Hope, Crosby and Lamour teamed up to make *The Road to Utopia*. Frank Butler was still behind the scenes, but Don Hartman was no longer an associate. Although funny in spots, *Utopia* was no *Morocco*, which even today plays hilarious on late night television showings.

The plot of *Utopia* was typical *Road*, the recipe of which was once defined by Crosby this way: "The basic ingredient of any 'Road' picture is a Rover Boys type plot, plus music. The plot takes two fellows, throws them into a jam or as many jams as possible, then lets them clown their way out. The jams are plotted in the script, and although they're bogus situations and on the incredible side, they're important because they hold the story together and provide a framework for our monkeyshines."

Utopia was set in frigid Alaska, rather than a tropical clime as was used in previous *Road* movies. Lacking the full-scale comic richness of a *Morocco*, *Utopia* still notched its share of hilarious moments. The classic and best recalled scene is Hope's encounter with a grizzly bear. Mistaking the bear for a fur-clad Lamour, Hope attempts to propose, promising: "I'll do things for you—big things—after we're married." Taking the bear's paw tenderly, he observes: "Dear, you've been working too hard." Pressing his suit, Hope makes this offer. "We'll go and live with my folks," he says. The bear then growls fiercely, prompting Hope to make this counter offer, "All right, then—*your* folks."

Utopia could have been funnier, but a decision had been made to incorporate a narrator in the film. He was humorist Robert Benchley, a funnyman with impeccable writing credentials. Unfortunately, his comments on the film action proved distracting and hampered its flow.

Despite a hackneyed plot, Hope managed several opportunities to ably display his vaunted false courage. Sauntering up to a grimy bar patronized by tough, weatherbeaten Yukon thugs, Hope orders a drink, a lemonade. Quickly realizing he'll be taken for a weak-kneed slicker, he adds: "In a dirty glass."

There is a lighthearted stab at satire at one point in the movie when a freezing, ice-capped mountain peak is transformed into the Paramount trademark—a towering mountaintop with a star around it.

Utopia is also remembered for the unusual plot twist that comes in the last scene of the film. Hope has won Lamour and the camera pans a cozy domestic scene some twenty years later. The contented middle-aged couple is visited by an equally middle-aged Crosby, who had once been a determined rival for Lamour.

The small talk of the past turns to a mention of the couple's son. The camera zooms in for a closeup of a photograph of the son. Revealed is a young man who bears an unmistakable resemblance to Crosby!

Bob in trouble in Louisiana Purchase (1941)

Victor Moore and Vera Zorina co-starred with Bob in Louisiana Purchase

Madeleine Carroll was Bob's "favorite blonde", Gale Sondegaard and George Zucco were the villains (My Favorite Blonde, 1942)

By 1948, when the fifth *Road* picture was made, Hope was nearing the peak of his film career. *The Road to Rio* also is ranked by many movie buffs as the peak of the *Road* series.

Its plot concerns a rich and beautiful heiress played by Dorothy Lamour, who is being duped into a marriage for money. The devious scheme to separate Lamour from her legacy has been engineered by her money-hungry aunt, played convincingly by Gale Sondergaard. The two gentlemen to the rescue who attempt to foil the foul flimflam are Hope and Crosby.

The film has a fair quota of desperate situations and perilous circumstances, and the crazy adventures are deftly adapted to the exotic atmosphere of the South American capital city. There is a lavish wedding scene featuring a sidesplitting musical routine with Hope dressed as a Carmen Miranda character. This is a baldfaced burlesque of the standard dance spectacular highlighting all Latin American–type Hollywood musicals.

In *Rio* Hope wins top honors once again in his amorous pursuit of the leading lady. His victory is abetted by subterfuge. Lamour's aunt had attempted to use hypnosis to gain control of the family fortune. Hope uses the same approach to win Lamour's love. The post-hypnotic suggestion works perfectly.

A bewildered Crosby learns later why Hope got the girl only when he tails the happy couple to a Niagara Falls honeymoon retreat. Peering through their bedroom-door keyhole, Crosby sees Hope dangling a gleaming pendant before Lamour's inanimate eyes. She wilts before his very eye.

An added starter in *Rio* were the Andrews sisters, who had been more familiar to movie-goers in "B" pictures. They were given the roles as a result of their association with Crosby on records. Crosby and the trio sang "You Don't Have to Know the Language."

Five years later producers managed to corral a busy Hope and Crosby long enough to shoot the sixth entry in the *Road* series, *The Road to Bali*.

From the beginning Dorothy Lamour had been the most frequent target of critical brickbats for her *Road* roles. After seeing *Road to Singapore*, Frank Nugent in the *New York Times* pinpointed her shortcomings: "Odd, in a way, the things Miss Lamour can do to a comedy, the reason being, we suppose, that Miss Lamour is no comedienne."

Although many thought her talents lay in other areas, and it is true that as the series continued the scripts were tailored more to

Bob and Madeleine Carroll in My Favorite Blonde (1942)

Hope and Crosby, she remained a perfect foil. Each succeeding role cemented her part in the *Road* mystique. For many fans it had become unthinkable to film a *Road* movie without her. Even though she was no longer under contract to Paramount she was given the lead in *Road to Bali*.

Bali made no pretense at being anything but a vehicle for Hope and Crosby to demonstrate their zany antics. With the exception of *Singapore*, the first *Road* flick in the series, both played out-of-work show business types. In *Bali* they're vaudeville actors, which is what they were in *Morocco* and *Utopia*. In *Zanzibar* and *Rio* they were unemployed carnival performers.

Bali's plot serves strictly as a blueprint for constructing gags and improbable situations. As usual Hope and Crosby are running away. As usual they just happen to be blessed with incredible luck by getting stranded on a beautiful and exotic island paradise. As usual Dorothy Lamour (Princess Lalah) reigns as the revered sovereign.

The ethnic strains of her loyal subjects are expediently diverse and include a melting pot of Apache Indians, Hollywood stars and stunning but stupid chorus girls. For intrigue there's the regular villain. This time he's an evil prince whose mission is the theft of the sunken treasure. Fortunately for the paying customers, Hope and Crosby ignored the trite plot, indulging fully and freely in their typical repartee.

They continue their wary friendship. The mutual distrust, which is the unifying element of their unusual relationship, is restated in a scene in which Crosby promises: "I've got a dame lined up for you."

"A dame?" replies the suspicious Hope. "What's wrong with her?"

Girl-chaser and goldbrick Hope reinforces these dubious but recurring aspects of his screen reputation by commenting: "I haven't looked for work since I was a night watchman at Vassar."

Often the simulated feud centered on Hope's envy of Crosby's ability to sing. As Crosby prepares to rumble into song at one point, Hope turns to the audience and warns: "He's going to sing, folks—now's the time to go and get the popcorn." Later on, Hope denounces Crosby by sputtering: "You collapsible Como, you."

Throughout Hope's career in all areas of show business, he often resorted to self-deprecating humor mocking his self-acclaimed image as a dashing lady's man. A perfect example of the technique came in *Bali*. After being smacked in the face repeatedly by branches during a harrowing jungle trek, he complains: "I haven't been smacked this much since my first rumble seat."

Bob fell for Madeleine Carroll in My Favorite Blonde—It's Bob's favorite role

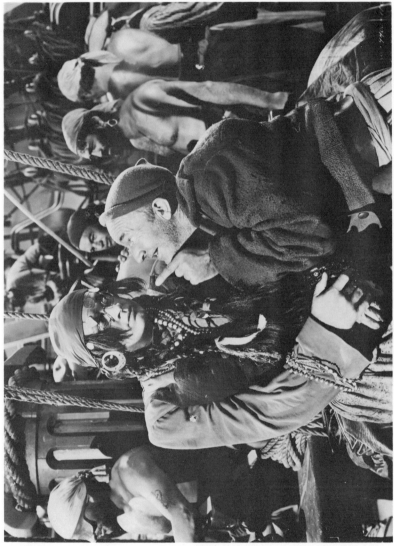

Bob and Walter Brennan starred for Sam Goldwyn in The Princess and the Pirate (1944)

Bali was not preoccupied with plot, so it was fairly easy to work a number of stars into the script in cameo roles. Included were Jane Russell, Dean Martin and Jerry Lewis, Bob Crosby and Humphrey Bogart. Miss Russell appears in a magical basket filled with several other equally lucious ladies. In the short scene, all are lured from the basket by the magnetic pied-piping of Hope.

Bogart had just won the Academy Award for best actor in *The African Queen*. His connection with that film is exploited in *Bali* by showing him hauling a boat through a swamp, which is what he did as the leading character in the most dramatic sequence in *Queen*.

Another gag involving Bogart comes when he forgets his Oscar during a mirage scene. Crosby has picked it up and Hope snatches it away snapping, "Give me that—you've already got one." (Crosby had won the Oscar in 1946 for his compelling performance as a priest in *Going My Way*.)

Hope's attitude toward the Oscar he's never received for his acting has always been used as a topic of humor. In *Morocco* he rebukes Crosby for interrupting his death speech, saying: "Aw gee, why'd you have to spoil the only big scene I've got in the picture? I might've won an Academy Award."

In *Bali* Hope indulges in an amusing Oscar fantasy while on the run from alligators. He imagines what his big moment would be like and preens himself like a cat in anticipation. He pretends to attend to his makeup, nervously smoothing his eyebrows with a moistened finger. A final check and he's ready for his acceptance speech. "Friends, this is a proud moment for me, receiving this Academy Award. I'd like to say one word ... "

But even the make-believe Oscar proves elusive. His speech and daydreaming are abruptly halted by the shouted alarm that the alligators have returned.

Hope's characteristic cowardice when confronted by ticklish situations provides many of the laughs in *Bali*. In one threatening tangle, Crosby advises Hope to "Keep cool." "Cool," he replies. "I'm numb." In another scrape his cowardly horror of physical pain is underscored when he blurts: "I can't stand torture. It hurts!"

But true to form, the ultimate horror for bachelor Hope is not pain but matrimony. Captured by cannibals in one scene, he quickly discerns that he's earmarked as an entrée. He attempts to play down his devourability by pleading, "I'm skinny—stringy."

But when a gap-toothed, matronly and amorous lady native with designs on Hope as a mat-mate responds, saying "No—you're going

Hope befriended in The Princess and the Pirate

127

to be married!" he switches tactics and implores the chef to "Go ahead! Eat me! I'm fat."

In the face of danger, the wily pair of ne'er-do-well picaresque tramps often resort to gimmicks to escape a brush with death. Since they portray vaudeville players between bookings in *Bali*, they resurrect the old vaudeville patty-cake gambit, which they had used with great results in most of the other *Road* films. The routine is naked slapstick in which the two momentarily divert the attention of their assailants by launching into a children's patty-cake game.

The sight of two grown men playing patty-cake forces whoever is chasing the pair into a dumbfounded, slack-jawed paralysis, whereupon Hope and Crosby close their slapping hands into fists and deliver knockout punches. In *Road to Hong Kong* a variation of the patty-cake routine is used. The two beefy characters chasing Hope and Crosby see them go into their windup and promptly flatten them, saying: "We saw the other movies, pal."

The presence of danger also forced a temporary halt to the mutual insults commonly exchanged between Hope and Crosby. At one tense moment, Hope confesses with some regret: "I know I must have been a trial to you."

But once they're out of danger and Crosby has won Lamour, Hope resumes the offensive with the crack, "How nearsighted can you be?"

Since there was a five-year interval between *Rio* and *Bali*, both the public and the critics affectionately rejoiced in the return of the make-believe prodigal rascals. Bosley Crowther led the formal welcome-back reception by declaring: " ... and now that they're back in 'Road to Bali' ... the outrage of their collective absence is just beginning to sink in."

The inspiration for the *Road* pictures ran out in 1962 when the grand finale in the series, *The Road to Hong Kong*, was made. Twenty-two years had somehow slipped by and the sharp-witted lovers of the forties had become aging lotharios. Time proved to be the toughest critic of all.

Initially it was reported by columnist Louella Parsons that Hope and Crosby would not use Dorothy Lamour as their love interest.

Parsons theorized that Lamour was to be dropped from the proposed picture because she was considered too old for the role of leading lady, despite the fact that she was younger than Bob and Bing. The columnist felt that Lamour was a vital ingredient in the magical *Road* mixture, and she bluntly criticized Hope and Crosby

Dorothy Lamour was his "Favorite Brunette" (1947)

Peter Lorre and Lon Chaney were among the bad guys in My Favorite Brunette

for permitting the decision to drop Dorothy to even be considered. In the face of such powerful pressure, both men wisely decided it would be foolish to buck the Lamour tide.

While eventually Dorothy made a guest appearance, her customary role as the love interest was filled by Joan Collins, a sexy, well-built actress who possessed the body of the 1940's version of Lamour.

Other guest shots were made by Peter Sellers, Frank Sinatra, Dean Martin, David Niven, Zsa Zsa Gabor and Jerry Colonna.

Judging both plot and performance, *Hong Kong* was by far the poorest *Road* picture. Both Hope and Crosby were unable to disguise the fact that they were simply going through the motions.

An updated space age plot centers on a mathematical formula, which represents the sum total of all mathematics from Copernicus to Einstein. A cadre of ruthless power-seekers, led by Robert Morley, eagerly press to obtain the secret formula before the United States or Russia. The story twist is that Hope has absorbed all the numbers but has suffered amnesia. Joan Collins at first is part of the villainous conspiracy, but then she defects to help Hope and Crosby. The standard series of madcap adventures is routinely covered in launches into outer space and chases into the underworld.

Compared with the fireworks in *Rio* or *Morocco, Hong Kong* was a comic dud. As if they realized they were in a clinker, the stars at one point openly allude to that possibility. Lamour asks Hope and Crosby in an aside, "Is that the plot of the picture so far?" They nod and she says, "I'd better hide you."

"From the killers?" they ask. "No," she responds. "The critics!"

This attempt to lampoon the film's glaring flaws was too accurate to be funny. This last one for the road turned out to have been one too many.

The *New York Times* critic wrote: "All in all, you felt they enjoyed getting together again, and you wish them well. The effect on screen is rather embarrassing, however."

Archer Winston of the *New York Post* softened the truth and noted kindly: "Give them all an 'A' for effort; then suit yourself about attending."

Although in aggregate the *Road* series played uneven, all the films were financial successes. *Time* magazine once estimated that the seven films earned a total of $50 million throughout the world. *Utopia* and *Rio* rank among the five top money-makers of Hope's film career, with domestic grosses of $4.5 million each.

Bob and Dottie in My Favorite Brunette

Since most of the *Road* pictures were part of Paramount's concession to the inroads of television, millions of Americans too young to have seen them in theatres when they were first released have caught them in recent years at home.

Bali and *Rio* were not in the original Paramount package of its early films sold to TV because Hope and Crosby had had the foresight to obtain two-thirds of the distribution rights to both movies.

In retrospect, much of the box-office appeal and success of the *Road* movies may be attributed to the feeling of sheer fun that Hope, Crosby and Lamour easily conveyed to the audiences. Often the three have reminisced publicly about the great fun they had filming the series.

Their collective merriment (they obviously reveled in each other's company) pervades each film and survives even today when many of Hope's topical remarks do not. Looking back now, some of the funniest scenes occurred when the script was ignored in favor of Hope's and Crosby's improvisations.

Undoubtedly, the spontaneity was the underlying reason for the cast's unrestrained enjoyment, which at times was electrically transmitted from studio to screen. Even the animals got into the act. In *Morocco*, for instance, the cameras were reeling away when a camel, with absolutely no prompting from Crosby, spat in Hope's eye. Apparently, the merriment was contagious. This became a funny bit in a very funny movie.

After *Zanzibar*, Hope starred in the political comedy *Lousiana Purchase*, an undistinguished film. His next film, *My Favorite Blonde* (1942), with Madeleine Carroll, began a three-part series of spy pictures. Hope once remarked that his role as Larry Haines, the vaudeville performer who befriends Miss Carroll, was his all-time film favorite because, "it permitted a great deal of variety in acting . . ."

Hope explained his feeling this way:

> Until I played in this picture, my comedy scenes had been getting broader and broader; so, although I was perfectly willing to do broad stuff, I liked the fact that in "My Favorite Blonde" I wasn't limited to slapstick and double takes.
>
> Too, this picture spread its humor nicely. Some scripts have big comedy scenes at the start, then the pace dips for about forty minutes, and there's another big laugh routine at the end. For my money, a comedy should build up like a rolling snowball, instead of sagging in the middle like an aging mattress.

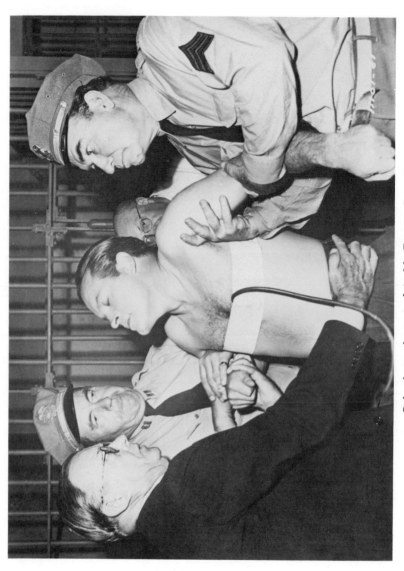

Bob, always the coward, in My Favorite Brunette

Patrick Knowles, Hope, Cecil Kellaway in Monsieur Beaucaire (1946)

Many of the Hope character traits so manifest in the *Road* films are depicted with equal frequency in *Blonde*. His unconcealed admiration for Miss Carroll and her just as concealed admiration for him inspire some of Hope's traditional wry comments on his lack of sex appeal. One remark comes in a scene in which she uses him as a human shield and he mistakes her grab for the real thing.

"I thought for a change a girl was trying to pick me up," he muses sadly.

In another scene he ruefully confesses: "I've stopped kissing strange women." When asked what's stopping him, he replies: "Strange women."

Blonde also offered Hope many opportunities to demonstrate his pose as a quick wit and an empty wallet.

At one particularly harrowing moment in a nerve-jangling chase scene, Miss Carroll asks Hope, "Do you know what it feels like to be watched and hounded every second?"

A true egocentric, he answers: "I used to, but now I pay cash for everything."

Money, rather Hope's lack of it, helps bring off another funny line when he protests indignantly over his rough handling at the hands of the authorities. "They can't do this to me, I'm an American citizen. I pay taxes. [Short pause] Well, I'm an American citizen."

Confronted by the villains, Hope the hero-but-confirmed-coward implores Miss Carroll to flee with him. "Let's get out of here before my knees beat each other to death," he chatters.

In the climactic chase scene (most of Hope's films had one) Miss Carroll urges him to step on it. Lacking her reckless abandon, he responds: "We haven't got wings, you know—but we soon may have."

His admission at the close of the story that "I'd do it all over again even if I were in my right mind," illustrates the standard Hope explanation for his role of reluctant hero.

Hope was never noted for being a physical comedian (i.e., acrobatic pratfalls), but one of his favorite comic ploys is the use of outlandish garb. Many of the *Road* movies feature Hope clad in grass skirts, or in other types of women's clothing. In *Blonde* Hope dresses as a penguin in an animated duet with Percy the Penguin. Percy sings Hope's theme song, "Thanks for the Memory." When the bird gets more applause than he does, Hope inquires: "You got relatives out there?" Finally, Hope threatens: "You and me'll have to have a talk with a taxidermist."

Bob as the barber, Beaucaire; Valentino played the part in the silent version

In 1947 Hope teamed with Dorothy Lamour to make *My Favorite Brunette*. The story was based on a format similar to *Blonde*. Hope played a baby photographer who bumbled his way through a probe of an international combine engaged in a uranium conspiracy.

As in *Cat and the Canary*, *Ghostbreakers* and *My Favorite Blonde*, Hope is an amateur sleuth who stumbles through a farcial melodrama played for laughs. While funny, the movie is inferior to *Blonde*, since the entire comic burden is placed on Hope. Some critics thought Miss Lamour had little of the instinctive flair for comedy Miss Carroll had.

In *Brunette* there is one funny sequence where Dorothy is trying to get information from him. "C'mon—tell me, tell me—C'mon, tell me—C'mon—" Suddenly she lowers her voice and says: "Come on, tell it to Mama." Hope's double take was priceless. Lamour and Bob worked well together, despite the critics' lack of regard for her comedy talents.

The reviews of *Brunette* were raves. Typical was Howard Barnes's glowing opinion, which appeared in the *Herald Tribune*. "The Edmund Beloin-Jack Rose script is funny, but it would prove somewhat labored were it not for the star's brilliant realization of each zany situation. Here is a comedian of great stature. ... Performing such as this is no trick. It is high artistry," he wrote.

My Favorite Spy, made in 1951, is a sparkling comedy with Hedy Lamarr as the love interest. Again, Hope is the amateur caught in a web of intrigue. His foes are cold-blooded villains. Miss Lamarr supplies the warmth.

The story hinges on the adage that everyone has a perfect double. Hope plays veteran burlesque comic Peanuts White, whose lookalike is super-spy Eric Augustine. Hope's assignment is to impersonate the infamous undercover genius and steal a piece of microfilm containing plans for a global pilotless plane. The trail of the secret plans leads to Tangier and Miss Lamarr, who plays Lily Dalbray, a beautiful and talented spy who has worked with Augustine on other capers.

Much of the fun in *Spy* derives from Hope's inept attempts to impersonate the suave, sophisticated and debonaire Augustine. After he's been captured by the other side, Hope is injected with truth serum. He is thought to be Augustine and the opposition believes they have been double-crossed by him. Their attempt to pry open his mind backfires when Hope starts babbling about his career in burlesque. He does a hammy one-man rendition of *Uncle Tom's Cabin*.

Hope's biggest hit, The Paleface, (1948) with Jane Russell

Lucille Ball, Mary Jane Saunders, Hope: Sorrowful Jones (1949)

140

Hope the coward emerges for the full treatment. In one scene, chilled with fear, he smacks his numbed arms and orders: "Get in there, blood."

The chase scene utilizes a fire engine in one of the best mad scrambles in a Hope film. Miss Lamarr and Hope are being held as prisoners in a private house. When she becomes convinced Hope has been telling her the truth, she sets fire to it. In the confusion they escape, but only to wander into the fire house where the firemen are rushing to respond to the alarm. Somehow the couple winds up perched precariously on the fire engine during the mad dash to the blaze site.

Hope managed to find time to make other movies in addition to the *Road* and *Favorite* series. In 1941 he made a war comedy, *Caught in the Draft*. In 1942 he was extremely busy with *Morocco* and *Blonde*, both top-notch comedies. In 1943 he wandered through the very mediocre *They Got Me Covered*, a Goldwyn, RKO production that sought to be an espionage farce set to music. Later in the year, he slipped through the filming of another wartime comedy, *Let's Face It*. He played GI Jerry Walker in a casual performance that is recalled only for its topical quips, such as:

●She looks like Veronica Lake with two eyes.

●Whatever happened to Wilkie?

●Wait till the paper-hanger hears about this (a comment made to a German prisoner about Hitler).

In 1944 Hope made *The Princess and the Pirate*, which co-starred Virginia Mayo. Of little import, the swashbuckling farce featured Hope as Sylvester the Great, a trick entertainer. The costumed, period-type story line continued to attract Hope, and in 1946 he made *Monsieur Beaucaire*. As a dashing barber to the royal court, Hope is bewigged and beruffled, but all for naught because the overall effect of the film is contrived and artificial.

Hope's last costume picture was *Casanova's Big Night*, which was filmed in 1954. Hope plays Pippo Poppoline, a tailor's apprentice who masquerades as the Great Lover. The rich Duchess of Genoa hires Hope to test the virtue of her prospective daughter-in-law. A lavish production co-starring Joan Fontaine and Basil Rathbone, the film hangs by the single thread of Hope's ability to impersonate Casanova.

Hope has the usual series of incredible adventures on his journey to Venice to complete his task as tempter. But as with the previous

Bob trying to outwit Bruce Cabot and Thomas Gomez in Sorrowful Jones

costume pictures, they are contrived and all too easily anticipated. The film hits a new low and the quip by Hope, "I can only only work two canals a day," is the highest moment of fun in the very below par outing.

The year 1948 was one that featured two brilliant film successes for Hope. The two smash hits were *The Road to Rio* and *The Paleface. Paleface* was the biggest solo triumph in Hope's motion picture career. It grossed approximately $4.5 million and sent him to the top of the box-office popularity charts. In his most famous role, as Painless Peter Potter, a dentist, Hope weds Calamity Jane, portrayed by a stacked Jane Russell.

Paleface represents Hope at the top of his bumbling, cowardly form. This outrageously funny parody of the standard Hollywood horse opera offers the full array of Hope's celebrated screen characteristics.

Brandishing a cloak of false bravado, Hope struts boldly into a saloon only to be knocked off his feet by the swinging doors. Barely able to swallow the head off the pint of beer, he quickly recovers, saying: "Never mind the chaser." His courage is called into question and he is forced to prove himself by gulping "four fingers of rye." He tells the barkeep to add the "thumb" for good measure. He tosses the potent drink down, and then asks pugnaciously: "Got nuthin' stronger, huh?" But then the liquor hits him like a shotgun blast, his eyes bug out, his body shudders and his hard-guy pose is shattered in a wave of derisive laughter.

Femme fatale Jane Russell is an ideal unliberated nineteenth-century old-West sex object, a robust woman in a region where the men are men and the women are proud of it. She's an ideal foil for Hope's exuberant lust. At their first meeting, Hope observes: "Now I know what Horace Greeley meant."

Hope is all wolf and no finesse, and his attempts at love-making are invariably terminated by his being knocked unconscious. Miss Russell punctuates their kisses with knockout blows from her gun butt. Unaware of her treachery in the clinch, Hope is sure of his amatory success. At one point he spots a corpse on the floor as he's making his pitch, and asks her: "Is that another of the guys you've kissed?"

Unlike many other of Hope's films, *Paleface* did not rely on the endless string of gags to sustain its humor. The writers skillfully incorporated many of the features of the standard western thriller to sustain the action. There are the expected band of vengeful Indians,

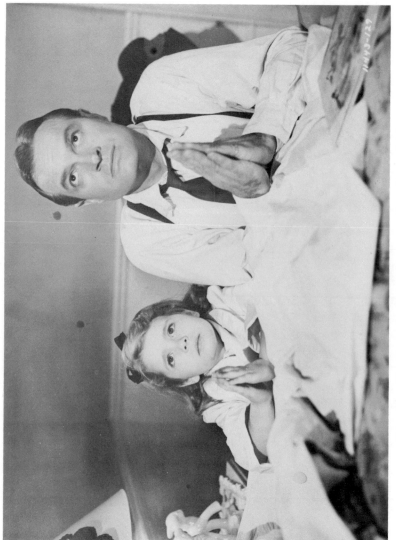

Mary Jane Saunders wins Bob over; a scene from Sorrowful Jones

Paramount reteamed Lucy and Bob for Fancy Pants (1950)

an exciting battle featuring runaway horses and the explosive use of dynamite.

Hope's capture by the Indians provides the most hilarous scene in the film. He is tied to a pair of bent, straining, supple trees. Facing the certain prospect of being torn in two, he can't resist the chance to assure one of his captors: "You'll get your half."

The satire is brilliantly depicted in the film's featured song, "Buttons and Bows," sung by Hope, who accompanies himself on the concertina. The song, when recorded by Dinah Shore, became a sensational popular hit and remained number one in the record charts for over six months. Since that time it has become a standard part of Hope's repertoire along with "Thanks for the Memory" and "It's De-Lovely." Some of Hope's more dogged critics assert that these are the only three songs he knows by heart, a pointed reference to Hope's increasing dependence on cue cards.

Though *Paleface* was a huge box-office success, the critics were divided. Bosley Crowther of the *New York Times* panned the film by saying it was "just another amusing run through of well worn slapstick routines by a boy who has bunions on his bunions from the number of times he's run the course." But Howard Barnes felt Hope was up to par and wrote, "Rarely has he been so funny."

The success of *Paleface* led to a sequel, *Son of Paleface*, made in 1952. Surprisingly, it is every bit as funny as its predecessor. Instead of a dentist, Hope plays a Harvard man.

Junior is an Ivy Leaguer, a son of the golden West, who returns to Sawbuck Pass to claim the fortune he believes his father has stashed away for him. Jane Russell plays Mike, a saloon singer concealing her true identity as the Torch, a lady bandit. When Miss Russell takes a fancy to Junior (Hope), the college boy becomes embroiled in several touchy scrapes with her, averting disaster only with the timely aid of Roy Rogers and his faithful horse Trigger.

The plot is simply delightful nonsense that prevails throughout the picture. Hope, perched atop a gas buggy and dressed like a city-slicker in a duster and goggles and a white wool varsity sweater that has a massive letter "H" sewn on the chest, returns to the roughhewn town of swinging doors and spittoons where he was born.

His arrival signals the beginning of an unrelenting merry spoof of western movies. Roy Rogers leaps aboard a speeding stagecoach in the most difficult, most flamboyant manner imaginable when it is obvious there is a far easier way. Trigger does a comedy bit too,

His billing was: Paramount presents Mr. Robert Hope (formerly Bob) in Fancy Pants

pulling the covers off Hope in one scene. Another animal gag involved a flock of performing buzzards.

Hope the screen coward stoops to an all-time low when he gets in a nasty jam with a senior citizen. "If you weren't as old and weak as you are ... you are old and weak aren't you? Then put up your dukes!" Hope growls.

But the grizzled old saddle-tramp is not as old as Hope is weak and Hope is flattened. At another point in the action even Hope's false bravado deserts him. Told that the color has left his cheeks, he admits: "I know. My blood's gone down to my hip pocket to count my money."

Hope makes an appropriate effort to sample the wares of Miss Russell in a number of scenes. His lascivious passes are too blunt to be successful. He invites her to "stroll around the rock quarry" and then tells her, "In college I majored in geology, anthropology and running out of gas on Bunker Hill." One potent Russell kiss causes Hope to levitate in an upright stance while his spurs spin around wildly.

Covering all his comic bases, Hope continues his simulated feud with Bing Crosby in this reference to the multimillionaire singer: "He's just an old broken down character actor on the Paramount lot: we try to keep him working."

The comedy in *Son of Paleface* is perfectly complemented by the rousing presentation of several lively musical numbers. Jane Russell and her dance hall dollies join for an ensemble routine entitled "Wing Ding Tonight," a typical western movie hoedown. Later, Roy Rogers leaves Trigger long enough to croon "California Rose" and an outlandish burlesque of the inevitable western movie ballad, "There's a Cloud in My Valley of Sunshine." Hope, Russell and Rogers join for a bouncier rendition of "Buttons and Bows" than the version that was used in *Paleface*, an acknowledgment of sorts that the song deserved better treatment than it first received.

In 1949 Hope starred in *Sorrowful Jones*, a remake of the Damon Runyon favorite, *Little Miss Marker*, which had starred Shirley Temple. With Lucille Ball as co-star, Hope played the hard-boiled, cynical bookie who accidentally becomes the guardian of a little girl, a role handled deftly by Mary Jane Saunders. Hope's decision to play surrogate father is influenced by his hopes that he can beat a racing commission investigation of his affairs by using the Good Samaritan act.

Hope and his cronies have bet a bundle on a pony slated to run in

Hope's first attempt at screen drama: The Seven Little Foys (1955)

His third "favorite" film: Bob with Hedy Lamarr in My Favorite Spy *(1951)*

Hope in The Seven Little Foys

the big race. They place the bet in the little girl's name to throw the gumshoes off their scent. The little girl's real father has been murdered by hoods. The hoods are after Hope and his young charge. A detective is after all of them.

The film makes a half-hearted attempt to be faithful to the tone of Runyon's famous and endearing yarn, but Hope wavers in his portrayal of the iron-willed Jones. In the scenes where the script and the direction have remained true to Runyon's story, Hope is obviously uncomfortable. He appears to be happier tossing off the gags written especially for the remake.

But the film was a big box-office hit and the critics were equally enthusiastic. Howard Barnes of the *Herald Tribune* opened his review with the statement: "Bob Hope is at his clowning best in 'Sorrowful Jones.'"

The remake of *Little Miss Marker* was such a surprise hit that Paramount repeated the formula one year later in *Fancy Pants*.

This film is based on Harry Leon Wilson's novel, *Ruggles of Red Gap*, which had weathered three previous screen versions: In 1918 Essanay made the film with Taylor Holmes; in 1923 Paramount remade it with Edward Everett Horton; and in 1935 the same company brought it out once again with Charles Laughton. For Hope's version, Paramount decided to stay with his *Sorrowful Jones* movie mates, Lucille Ball and Bruce Cabot. Hope plays Humphrey, a valet, but there's just too much slapstick in *Fancy Pants* to suit Hope's fancy. Physical comedy was never his forte, and the film is unquestionably substandard.

In 1951 Hope signed for a second film based on a Damon Runyon story, *The Lemon Drop Kid*. Another race track opus, it illustrates Hope's frequent penchant for making every movie a vehicle for launching his gags and one-liners. As with *Sorrowful Jones*, Runyon gets lost in the translation and the coherence of the tale gets watered down in a curious mixture of vintage Runyon and freshly pressed Hope.

Hope plays the title role of a hanger-on in the winner's circle who touts a powerful racketeer's moll off a winning nag and loses the mobster's friendship. The chieftain, named Moose Moran, also threatens Hope's life unless Hope makes good on the $10,000 worth of bad advice.

The plot consists mostly of Hope's ensuing frenzied efforts to raise the cash to guarantee his survival. The comic meandering includes brief segments that showcase Hope's inclination toward dressing up.

*Bob joins the "little old ladies" Spring Byington and Ida Moore in The Lemon Drop Kid
(1951)*

In one scene Hope dons a Santa Claus outfit and in another he transforms himself into a sixty-year-old doll.

Marilyn Maxwell plays Hope's girlfriend. They sing a lot together as the rest of the cast makes a vain attempt to appear as convincing recreations of Runyon's cheap Broadway hoods. In the final analysis, *The Lemon Drop Kid* dissolves into a sour failure because it lacks the creative nonsense so necessary to overcome the obvious flaws.

Throughout Hope's lengthy and prolific film career, he was often to be upset by criticism that he could not act, that in fact he simply played himself in every movie role. The comments angered him many times because he thought of himself as a professional who did his very best with the material at hand. But no doubt he yearned for a serious role, one which would prove beyond question that the self-appointed taste-makers were all wet.

In 1955 Hope took the plunge, departing from his customary portrayal of shallow, mindless nits to take on a serious dramatic assignment. He was cast as Eddie Foy in a Class-A first-line biographical musical comedy, *The Seven Little Foys*. The fact that Foy and his family had been a vaudeville institution, the segment of show business in which Hope got his start, must have played a major part in his decision to accept the role. The script was sculptured to fit all of his unique talents.

The film was a joint venture with three partners. They were Scribe Productions, an independent outfit owned by screenwriters Jack Rose and Mel Shavelson who had been gag men for Hope in radio, Paramount and Hope Enterprises.

The story was a slice of real life concerned chiefly with Foy's decision to launch a vaudeville team made up of himself and his seven children. It called for vaudeville-quality singing and dancing, two skills Hope had mastered before turning to laughs for money. In a dancing duet with James Cagney, who recreated his portrayal of George M. Cohan, done in an earlier film, Hope proved he had finally found the dramatic part to highlight his special talents.

To his delight he had not lost the skills he had worked so hard to acquire in the vaudeville days of the twenties. But he still worked hard to sharpen them. He rehearsed his dance numbers with Nick Castile for a month before actual shooting started. He was determined to be ready, just as he was determined to be good.

Foy was no real-life angel by any stretch of the imagination and the script thankfully resisted the urge to gloss over his faults by

153

Bob and Katharine Hepburn teamed for The Iron Petticoat *(1956)*

Hepburn and Hope in The Iron Petticoat

Pearl Bailey, Hope, Eva Marie Saint in That Certain Feeling (1956)

showing him as a scoutmaster-type family man. Foy's utter selfishness, which clung to him no matter what the circumstance, was depicted in a very frank scene that showed him enjoying a few belts at the Friars Club while his wife was dying in a hospital a few blocks away.

Foy's decision to go on stage with his kids is also portrayed realistically. The film's narrator, Eddie Foy, Jr., recalls: "He wanted as many kids between him and the audience as possible." There is an ample amount of Hope-type gags in the script, but it was said later that the humor lacked the endearing qualities needed to offset the cutting edge of the calculating side of Foy.

Hope's performance failed to gain the unanimous critical approval he no doubt had wished for. Bosley Crowther vaguely panned the film by saying that it might have sounded potentially amusing, "but it has an oddly unpleasant quality."

However, critic Wanda Hale of the *New York Daily News* spoke for the masses of the movie-going public when she raved: "Bob Hope doesn't have to take any more insults from Bing Crosby about his acting. Hope can now hold up his head with Hollywood's dramatic thespians as, for the first time in his career, Hope isn't playing Hope on the screen. He is acting and doing a commendable job."

Two years later Hope confounded the nitpickers in the critics' circle by mounting a stunning portrayal of New York City's most flamboyant City Hall scamp, Jimmy Walker, the East Side kid who became mayor. The script by Rose and Shavelson was based on the classic biography by the famous newspaperman Gene Fowler, an intimate of Walker's who entitled his reminiscences, *Beau James.*

Sticking with Fowler's apt title, the writers resisted the urge to flood the screen with an endless assortment of gags because Hope was playing the lead. Rose and Shavelson did not reproduce the *Foy's* formula, but rather made a serious attempt at a penetrating character study. For the most part they were successful.

Though depicted as an appealing rogue, Walker and his vices are graphically presented in full detail. For the first and only time in his film career, Hope found himself challenged with the task of playing the part of a real philanderer, rather than merely gliding through a counterfeit portrayal in fantasy.

At one point there is a line that sums up Walker's attitude toward his relationship with his wife, Allie, played by Alexis Smith. "Allie and I are united in the holy bonds of politics." Vera Miles does a

The kids love Bob: an atypical on-screen Hope situation in **That Certain Feeling**

magnificient job in the role of Betty Compton, one of Walker's more prominent other women.

The script does an admirable job of showing the casual attitude Walker felt toward his municipal responsibilities. He viewed the mayoralty as an irritating deterrent that often dampened his zest for the high life. His personal conception of his public office as everything but a public trust culminated in the famed Seabury probe, a massive investigation of city affairs that uncovered a seamy mess of rancid municipal graft.

One of the film's principal assets is its adroit use of humor to depict Walker's complex personality. After all, he was not a hack. He was a rogue, a slickster who knew at all times exactly what he was. In an election campaign scene, his keen awareness of the patronizing attitude that was commonly felt about his candidacy was revealed honestly in a retort to well-wishers who called him Mr. Mayor.

"Smile when you say that, everybody else does," Hope as Walker cracks.

When glaring headlines call for blood and force judges and officials on the take to flee the country, Hope, an island of detached calm in a sea of heat, quips: "Join the Party and see the world."

Toward the end of the movie, there is a scene in which Walker is seen at Yankee Stadium. His days of glory are over and the fans soundly boo him. Hope handles the poignant and dramatic moment skillfully, showing convincingly a Walker who could joke during the grimmest moments of his life.

"Maybe they think I'm going to umpire," he quips.

Hope's performance is touched with such mastery that he arouses sympathy in the scene where Walker is forced to hustle some money so he can buy a steamship ticket for his exile. Hope's portrayal of Walker's departure as a broken man from the city he loves constitutes a solid tour de force. One never stops to think that it's Hope. It's Walker in all his misery.

Beau James has several song and dance numbers which depict Walker's love of the nightside of New York City life. Jimmy Durante appears in the song-and-dance number, "His Honor, the Mayor of New York," which satirizes Walker as a chief executive. The mood of the period is painstakingly evoked, using the lyrics of Roger's and Hart's "Manhattan."

Remaining true to the time, the film also uses a song that was co-authored by Walker himself. It is entitled, "Will You Love Me in December?"

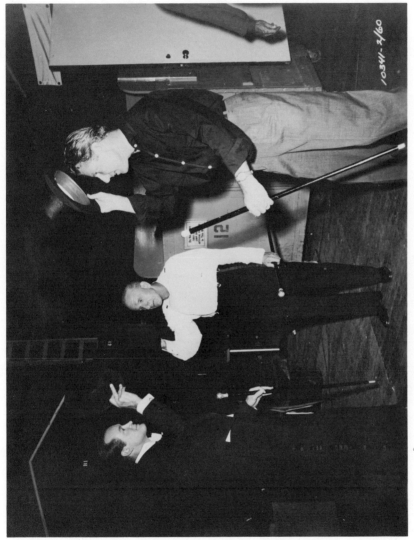

Bob and Jimmy Durante rehearsing for a scene in Beau James (1957)

Bob in drag in Casanova's Big Night (1954)

It is interesting to note that Hope and his writers, before the film was released, were concerned that the title would mislead the public into thinking it was a costume drama. After *Casanova's Big Night* and *Monsieur Beaucaire*, Hope knew that this misconception, if allowed to occur, would be deadly. Discussions of a title change were seriously considered. One alternative was *Will You Love Me in December?*. Editors and movie writers were polled before the final decison was reached. Maybe because Gene Fowler was one of their own, they opted for *Beau James* four to one. Hope and company respected the decision.

The preparation for the film, in light of its volatile subject matter, entailed considerable legal work. Three teams of lawyers reportedly spent six months obtaining the various releases required to bring Walker's colorful life to the screen. Money was paid to persons who figured in the screen version of Walker's life.

Cooperation came easily from unexpected quarters. Betty Compton's mother, the executrix of her late daughter's estate, was most reasonable. Her stipulations directed that her daughter's real name be used, and that the part be given to an actress who closely resembled her daughter.

In 1956, between *The Seven Little Foy's* and *Beau James*, Hope made *That Certain Feeling* and *Iron Petticoat*. The former was based on the Broadway play *King of Hearts*, written by Jean Kerr and Eleanor Brooke. It ranks among the most sophisticated and polished of Hope's seventy-plus films.

He plays Francis Y. Digman, a gifted but neurotic cartoonist who is unable to hold onto a job or onto his wife, beautifully portrayed by Eva Maria Saint. The role was far more complex than most of Hope's screen characterizations, and Hope was required to exercise more acting control than was his usual wont. *That Certain Feeling* is one of Hope's finest acting jobs and it demonstrates that given a good script and kept from employing his running stream of gags, Hope is adept in the more subtle aspects of comedy.

The script has a floodcrest of funny lines but they are integrated, not throw away gags. Hope's delivery reflects the nuances of Digman's wry viewpoint. As he is given a morning paper by his ex-wife, he comments with rueful nostalgia: "Not the first thing I reach for in the morning as you doubtless recall."

His sardonic attitude toward his rival, the suave and impeccable George Sanders, is reflected in his quips. His first look at Sanders's

Constantly in trouble: Hope as the famed lover in Casanova's Big Night

penthouse elicits the comment: "That's what I like—everything done in contrasting shades of money."

Hope's self-control totally deserted him in the *Iron Petticoat*. The film is an unmitigated disaster. Originally conceived as a *Ninotchka*-type farce co-starring Katharine Hepburn, the film disintegrated into a vehicle for Hope-type gags.

Ben Hecht, the highly regarded screenwriter, was so outraged by the ruthless mutilation of his script that he spent $275 for an ad on the back page of the *Hollywood Reporter* to tell Hope publicly what he thought.

The text was in the form of a letter. It read:

> My dear Partner Bob Hope:
> This is to notify you that I have removed my name as author from our mutilated venture, *The Iron Petticoat.*
> Unfortunately, your other partner, Katharine Hepburn, can't shy out of the fractured picture with me.
> Although her magnificent comic performance has been blow-torched out of the film, there is enough left of the Hepburn footage to identify her for her sharpshooters.
> I am assured by my hopeful predators that *The Iron Petticoat* will go over big with people "who can't get enough of Bob Hope."
> Let us hope this swooning contingent is not confined to yourself and your euphoric agent, Louis Shurr.
> [Signed] Ben Hecht

Hope replied by taking out an ad on the same page of a subsequent issue, in which he implied that since Hecht had left the film its financial and creative potential had been immeasurably strengthened. He signed his barb, "Bob (Blow-Torch) Hope."

From 1957 to 1972 Hope made close to twenty films, but with the notable exception of *The Facts of Life* in 1960 with Lucille Ball, their quality ranges from mediocre to miserable. *Paris Holiday*, made in 1958 with Anita Ekberg, is riddled with gags, supplied by Hope's stable of comedy writers, that fail to come off. *Bachelor in Paradise* in 1961 with Lana Turner was a box-office hit but the film has none of the zest usually associated with his good movies.

In *A Global Affair* in 1964 Hope was woefully miscast as a jaunty bachelor surrounded by a bevy of beautiful young girls. Hope was sixty-one when the film was released and while he appears in remarkably good shape, with the solid biceps of a man thirty years younger, it becomes readily apparent that there is only one Cary Grant.

Lovely Anita Ekberg joined Bob in Paris Holiday (1958)

Lucille Ball and Hope reteamed for the Facts of Life (1960)

Lucy and Bob in The Facts of Life

In *Facts of Life* Hope's co-star is Lucille Ball, his sidekick in *Sorrowful Jones* and *Fancy Pants*.

Hope is more plausible in this serious comedy, which explores the subject of adultery. His ability to quip his way out of tight spots is still intact. When Miss Ball is skeptical about his claiming painting as a hobby, he retorts: "What d' you want me to do—cut off my ear? It's a swell relaxation, less exhausting than beating the kids and almost as much fun."

He doesn't fare as well in *Critic's Choice* in 1963, the screen version of the sophisticated Broadway comedy by Ira Levin. Hope and co-star Lucille Ball are the fictional recreations of the famed drama critic Walter Kerr and his playwright wife, Jean. Hope's performance suffers badly when compared with Henry Fonda's Broadway portrayal.

Cancel My Reservation in 1972, which co-stars Eva Maria Saint in another shameful waste of her talent, follows the formula that proved to be so successful in the past. It's a comedy-mystery in which Hope and Miss Saint are cast as a husband-and-wife television talk team. On a vacation to obtain rest and escape from pressure, Hope becomes entangled in a murder case.

Hope is the prime suspect when the corpse of an Indian girl is found in his car. He and his wife spend the remainder of the film extricating him from the predicament and in the process resolving their testy marital dispute.

As customary in Hope's films, there are the featured cameo appearances, this time by such stars as Bing Crosby, Flip Wilson, John Wayne and Johnny Carson.

Cancel My Reservation was the first Hope film ever to be selected for a premiere at Radio City Music Hall, but it received a calamitous reception from the critics. Even the Rockettes were unable to muster any stir of interest at the ticket window. The evening before a strike by musicians closed the Music Hall, there were only 300 paying customers watching the movie in the massive auditorium, which seats 6,200 persons.

It is hoped that the scathing reviews will inspire Hope to come back in a fashion that will redeem his stature.

Filmography

1. *Going Spanish* (1934). Musical comedy short. Co-starring Leah Ray. Produced by Al Christie. Written by William Watson and

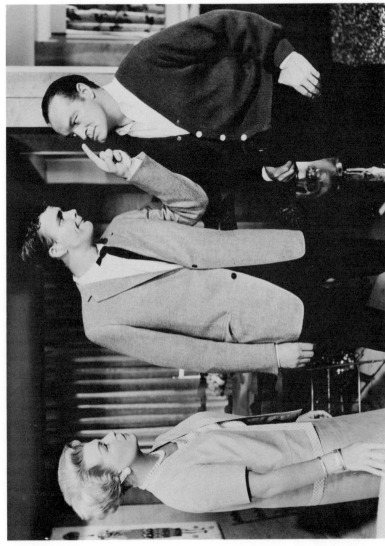

Lana Turner and Jim Hutton helped Hope with the laughs in Bachelor in Paradise (1961)

Art Jarrett. Educational Productions, Inc.

2. *Paree, Paree* (1934). Musical comedy short. With Dorothy Stone, Lorraine Collier, Charles Collins and Billie Leonard. Directed by Roy Mack. Written by Cyrus Wood. Warner Bros.

3. *The Old Gray Mayor* (1935). Comedy short. With Sam Wren, Ruth Blasco, Lionel Stander and George Watts. Directed by Lloyd French. Written by Herman Ruby. Warner Bros.

4. *Watch the Birdie* (1935). Wisecracking lover short. With George Watts, Arline Dinitz, Neil O'Day and Marie Nordstrom. Directed by Lloyd French. Written by Dolph Singer and Jack Henley. Warner Bros.

5. *Double Exposure* (1935). Sidewalk photog farce, short. With Loretta Sayers, Jules Epailly, Johnny Berkes. Directed by Lloyd French. Written by Burnet Hershey and Jack Henley. Warner Bros.

6. *Calling All Tars* (1936). Sailor suits make the man—and the girls too. Co-starring Johnny Berkes and Oscar Ragland. Directed by Lloyd French. Written by Burnet Hershey and Jack Henley. Warner Bros.

7. *Shop Talk* (1936). Inherit a department store, or, Son of Macy's. Short. Directed by Lloyd French. Written by Burnet Hershey and Jack Henley. Warner Bros.

8. *Don't Hook Now* (1938). A duffer competes as himself. Co-starring Bing Crosby. Directed by Herbert Poleise. Paramount.

9. *The Big Broadcast of 1938* (1938). As Buzz Fielding, the perennial emcee. With most of the Paramount contract players, including W. C. Fields, Martha Raye, Dorothy Lamour, Ben Blue, Leif Erickson, Leonid Kinskey, Patricia (Honey Chile) Wilder and a host of others. Directed by Mitchell Leisen. Written from a play about a book by Walter De Leon, Francis Martin and Ken Englund. Paramount.

10. *College Swing* (1938). Comedy with music. As Bub (Studyhard) Brady, who helps girl (Gracie Allen) pass her college entrance test. With George Burns, Ben Blue, Jerry Colonna, Robert Cummings, Cecil Cunningham, Jackie Coogan, Edward Everett Horton, Florence George, Betty Grable, Tully Marshall and John Payne. Directed by Raoul Walsh. Written by Walter De Leon and Francis Martin. Paramount.

11. *Give Me a Sailor* (1938). As naval officer Jim Brewster in love lightly. With Nana Bryant, Bonnie Jean Churchill, Edward Earle, Betty Grable, Clarence Kolb, Kathleen Lockhart, Martha

Bob was still a young bachelor (though sixty in real life) in A Global Affair *(1964)*

Bob and baby in A Global Affair

Bob, Rick Kellman and Jessie Royce Landis in Critic's Choice (1963)

Raye, Ralph Sanford, Emerson Treacy and Jack Whiting. Directed by Elliott Nugent. Written by Doris Anderson and Frank Butler. Paramount.

12. *Thanks for the Memory* (1938). Marriage on the rocks saved by a song. As novelist husband Steve Merrick. With Eddie "Rochester" Anderson, Charles Butterworth, William Collier, Sr., Laura Hope Crews, Emma Dunn, Edward Gargan, Roscoe Karns, Otto Kruger, Hedda Hopper, Jack Norton, Shirley Ross and Patricia (Honey Chile) Wilder. Directed by George Archainbaud. Written by Lynn Starling. Paramount.

13. *Never Say Die* (1939). Slapstick. As rich man John Kidley, a hypochondriac. With Ernest Cossart, Andy Devine, Paul Harvey, Alan Mowbray, Martha Raye, Siegfried Rumann. Directed by Elliott Nugent. Written by Frank Butler and Don Hartman. Paramount.

14. *Some Like It Hot* (1939). Comedy. As crazy concessionaire Nicky Nelson. With Sam Ash, Harry Barris, Rufe Davis, Richard Denning, Dudley Dickerson, Lillian Fitzgerald, Gene Krupa and Orchestra, Una Merkel, Bernard Nedell, Frank Sully, Pat West, Shirley Ross, Wayne "Tiny" Whitt and Clarence H. Wilson. Directed by George Archainbaud. Written by Lewis R. Roster and Wilkie C. Mahoney. Paramount.

15. *The Cat and the Canary* (1939). Farce. As Wally Hampton, mystery novel buff in real-life thriller. With John Beal, Paulette Goddard, Douglass Montgomery, Elizabeth Patterson, Willard Robertson, Gale Sondergaard, Nydia Westman and George Zucco. Directed by Elliott Nugent. Written by Walter De Leon and Lynn Starling. Paramount.

16. *Road to Singapore* (1940). Picaresque comedy. As Ace Lannigan, itinerant who hops slow boat to Far East with buddy (Bing Crosby) who's fleeing the altar. With Charles Coburn, Jerry Colonna, Bing Crosby, Dorothy Lamour and Anthony Quinn. Directed by Victor Schertzinger. Written by Frank Butler and Don Hartman. Paramount.

17. *The Ghostbreakers* (1940). Third of four versions of a super-natural murder mystery. As Larry Lawrence, radio reporter who's electrified in a haunted house. With Willie Best, Richard Carlson, Pedro De Cordoba, Tom Dugan, Paulette Goddard, Paul Lukas and Anthony Quinn. Directed by George Marshall. Written by Walter De Leon. Paramount.

18. *Caught in the Draft* (1941). Comedy. As Don Bolton, movie star,

Rip Torn was Bob's rival for Lucille Ball in Critic's Choice

in role as Army boot. With Irving Bacon, Eddie Bracken, Edgar Dearing, Paul Hurst, Clarence Kolb, Dorothy Lamour, Arthur Loft, Lynne Overman and Phyllis Ruth. Directed by David Butler. Written by Harry Tugend, with added dialogue by Wilkie C. Mahoney. Paramount.

19. *Nothing but the Truth* (1941). Comedy. As stockbroker Steve Bennett, who says he can't lie and lays $10,000 bet on it. With Glenn Anders, Edward Arnold, Willie Best, Catherine Doucet, Leif Erickson, Paulette Goddard, Clarence Kolb, Grant Mitchell and Helen Vinson. Directed by Elliott Nugent. Written by Ken Englund and Don Hartman from the play about the book. Paramount.

20. *Road to Zanzibar* (1941). Musical comedy. As carnival performer Fearless (Hubert) Frazier on safari. With Iris Adrian, Luis Alberni, Eric Blore, Bing Crosby, Douglas Dumbrille, Noble Johnson, Dorothy Lamour, Joan Marsh and Una Merkel. Directed by Victor Schertzinger. Written by Frank Butler and Don Hartman. Paramount.

21. *Louisiana Purchase* (1941). Comedy about politics. As Jim Taylor, attorney in a senatorial investigation. With Irene Bordoni, Barbara Britton, Frank Albertson, Dona Drake, Margaret Hayes, Donald MacBride, Victor Moore, Jack Norton, Maxie Rosenbloom, Phyllis Ruth, Raymond Walburn, Jean Wallace, Dave Willock and Vera Zorina. Directed by Irving Cummings. Written by Jerome Chodorov and Joseph Fields. Paramount.

22. *My Favorite Blonde* (1942). Spy comedy. As Larry Haines, vaudeville performer. His all-time favorite part. With Monte Blue, Madeleine Carroll, Edward Gargan, Isabel Randolph, Gale Sondergaard, Minerva Urecal, Victor Varconi, Dooley Wilson and George Zucco. Directed by Sidney Lanfield. Written by Frank Butler and Don Hartman. Paramount.

23. *The Road to Morocco* (1942). Desert spoof. As Turkey Jackson, vaudeville performer. With Monte Blue, Bing Crosby, Yvonne De Carlo, Dona Drake, Dorothy Lamour, Laura La Plante, Anthony Quinn and Mikhail Rasumny. Directed by David Butler. Written by Frank Butler and Don Hartman. Paramount.

24. *Star Spangled Rhythm* (1942). There's no business like the variety show business. Playing himself as emcee. With almost everyone, including Eddie Bracken, Walter Catlett, Bing Crosby, Cass Daley, Cecil B. De Mille, Paulette Goddard, Betty Hutton,

Bob helped pal Phyllis Diller's career with 8 on the Lam (1967)

Susan Hayward, Sterling Holloway, Alan Ladd, Veronica Lake, Gil Lamb, Dorothy Lamour, Diana Lynn, Victor Moore, Dick Powell, Anne Revere, Preston Sturges, Arthur Treacher and Ernest Truex. Directed by George Marshall. Written by Harry Tugend.

25. *They Got Me Covered* (1943). Spy comedy with songs. As Robert Kittredge, foreign correspondent. With John Abbott, Philip Ahn, Lenore Aubert, Florence Bates, Walter Catlett, Eduardo Ciannelli, Dorothy Lamour, Marion Martin, Donald Meek, Otto Preminger and Mary Treen. Directed by David Butler. Written by Harry Kurnitz. Goldwyn–RKO.

26. *Let's Face It.* (1943). Comedy about Army life. As dogface Jerry Walker. With Eve Arden, Dona Drake, Betty Hutton, Arthur Loft, Zasu Pitts, Phyllis Povah, Joseph Sawyer, Raymond Walburn, Marjorie Weaver and Dave Willock. Directed by Sidney Lanfield. Written by Harry Tugend. Paramount.

27. *Welcome to Britain* (1943). Short subject. As himself, explaining the British currency to American troops.

28. *The Princess and the Pirate* (1944). As swashbuckling magician Sylvester the Great. With Walter Brennan, Bing Crosby (cameo), Maude Eburne, Hugo Haas, Marc Lawrence, Mike Mazurki, Victor McLaglen, Virginia Mayo and Walter Slezak. Directed by David Butler. Written by Everett Freeman, Don Hartman and Melville Shavelson. Goldwyn–RKO.

29. *All Star Bond Rally* (1945). Filmed variety show in which Hope sings one song, "Buy Buy Bonds." You had to be there. Fox.

30. *Hollywood Victory Caravan* (1945). We won! Paramount.

31. *Road to Utopia* (1945). Comedy. As vaudeville actor Chester Hooton in the Yukon. With Robert Barrat, Robert Benchley (narrator), Hillary Brooke, Bing Crosby, Douglas Dumbrille, Dorothy Lamour, Jack La Rue and Nestor Paiva. Directed by Hal Walker. Written by Melvin Frank and Norman Panama. Paramount.

32. *Monsieur Beaucaire* (1946). As the barber of Madrid. With Hillary Brooke, Joan Caulfield, Constance Collier, Douglas Dumbrille, Cecil Kellaway, Patric Knowles, Mary Nash, Reginald Owen, Marjorie Reynolds and Joseph Schildkraut. Directed by George Marshall. Written by Melvin Frank and Norman Panama. Paramount.

33. *My Favorite Brunette* (1947). As amateur photog and sleuth Ronnie Jackson. With Lon Chaney, Jr., Charles Dingle, Ann

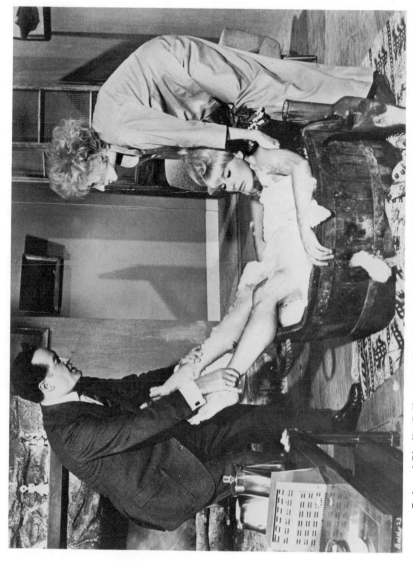

Bob and Phyllis Diller with Elke Sommer in Boy, **Did I Get a** *Wrong Number (1966). This was Hope's last big commercial film success, grossing $4 million*

Doran, Bing Crosby (cameo), John Hoyt, Dorothy Lamour, Peter Lorre, Frank Puglia and Willard Robertson. Directed by Elliott Nugent. Written by Edmund Beloin and Jack Rose. Paramount.

34. *Where There's Life* (1947). As Mike Valentine, disc jockey, who is left the keys to a kingdom. With John Alexander, William Bendix, George Coulouris, Signe Hasso, Dennis Hoey, Joseph Vitale, Harry Von Zell and George Zucco. Directed by Sidney Lanfield. Written by Allen Boretz and Melville Shavelson. Paramount.

35. *Variety Girl* (1947). Hope as Hope in a variety show. With Mary Hatcher, De Forest Kelley, Torben Meyer, Jack Norton, Olga San Juan and Nella Walker. Playing themselves Gary Cooper, Bing Crosby, Billy De Wolfe, Paulette Goddard, Alan Ladd, Burt Lancaster, Dorothy Lamour, Veronica Lake, Ray Milland, Robert Preston, Barbara Stanwyck and Gail Russell. Directed by George Marshall. Written by Monte Brice, Edmund Hartmann, Frank Tashlin and Robert Welch. Paramount.

36. *Road to Rio* (1948). As Hot Lips Barton, carny musician. With the Andrews Sisters, Jerry Colonna, Bing Crosby, Frank Faylen, Dorothy Lamour, Nestor Paiva, Frank Puglia, Gale Sondergaard, Joseph Vitale, Tad Van Brunt and the Wiere Brothers. Directed by Norman Z. McLeod. Written by Edmund Beloin and Jack Rose. Paramount.

37. *The Paleface* (1948). Western spoof. As Peter Potter, a dentist who marries Calamity Jane. With Stanley Adams, Iris Adrian, Robert Armstrong, Clem Bevans, Iron Eyes Cody, Jane Russell, Jack Searl, Charles Trowbridge, Joseph Vitale, Robert Watson and Jeff York. Directed by Norman Z. McLeod. Written by Edmund Hartmann and Jack Tashlin, with added lines by Jack Rose. Paramount.

38. *Sorrowful Jones* (1949). About a bookie and his little "ward." With Lucille Ball, Bruce Cabot, William Demarest, Thomas Gomez, Paul Lees, Tom Pedi and Mary Jane Saunders. Directed by Sidney Lanfield. Written by Edmund Hartmann, Jack Rose and Melville Shavelson, based on the Damon Runyon play *Little Miss Marker*. Paramount.

39. *The Great Lover* (1949). As boy scout leader Freddie Hunter afloat. With Sig Arno, Jim Backus, Roland Culver, Rhonda Fleming, Jackie Jackson, Jerry Hunter, Richard Lyon, George Reeves, Karl Wright and Roland Young. Directed by Alexander

Sexy Gina Lollobrigida joined in one of Hope's later frolics—The Private Navy of Sgt. O'Farrell (1968)

Hall. Written by Edmund Beloin, Jack Rose and Melville Shavelson. Paramount.

40. *Fancy Pants* (1950). As a valet named Humphrey. With John Alexander, Eric Blore, Bruce Cabot, Lucille Ball, Hugh French, Colin Keith-Johnston, Jack Kirkwood, Ida Moore, Lea Pennman, Norma Varden and Joseph Vitale. Directed by George Marshall. Written by Edmund Hartmann and Robert O'Brien. Paramount.

41. *The Lemon Drop Kid* (1951). Life as a tout is just a ten grand bet on a horse. With Harry Bellaver, Fred Clark, Jane Darwell, Jay C. Flippen, William Frawley, Andrea King, Marilyn Maxwell, Sid Melton and Ida Moore. Directed by Sidney Lanfield. Written by Edmund Hartmann, Robert O'Brien and Frank Tashlin. Paramount.

42. *My Favorite Spy* (1951). Double identity as Peanuts White, a burlesque comic lookalike for a spy, suave Eric Augustine. With Morris Ankrum, John Archer, Stephen Chase, Hedy Lamarr, Arnold Moss, Luis Van Rooten and Francis L. Sullivan. Directed by Norman Z. McLeod. Written by Edmund L. Hartmann and Jack Sher. Paramount.

43. *The Greatest Show on Earth* (1952). As a member of the circus audience in one unbilled crowd scene. Paramount.

44. *Son of Paleface* (1952). A sort of sequel as a Harvard man gone West. With Paul E. Burns, Iron Eyes Cody, Lloyd Corrigan, Douglas Dumbrille, Roy Rogers, Jane Russell, Trigger, Bill Williams and Harry Von Zell. Directed by Frank Tashlin. Written by Joseph Quillan, Frank Tashlin and Robert L Welch. Paramount.

45. *Road to Bali* (1953). As Harold Gridley, vaudeville song-and-dance man, tapping his way through the South Seas. With Leon Askin, Peter Coe, Bing Crosby, Dorothy Lamour, Ralph Moody and Murvyn Vye. As guests Bob Crosby, Jerry Lewis, Dean Martin and Jane Russell; Humphrey Bogart in film clip from *The African Queen*. Directed by Hal Walker. Written by Frank Butler, Hal Kanter and William Morrow. Paramount.

46. *Off Limits* (1953). As Wally Hogan, GI fight manager. With Stanley Clements, Carolyn Jones, Marilyn Maxwell, Eddie Mayehoff, Marvin Miller, John Ridgely, Mickey Rooney. Directed by George Marshall. Written by Hal Kanter and Jack Sher. Paramount.

47. *Here Come the Girls* (1953). As Stanley Snodgrass, the chorus

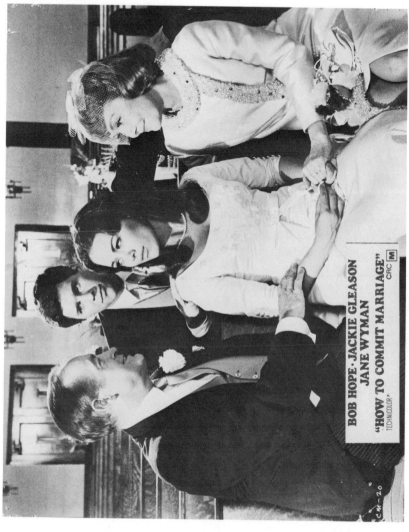

BOB HOPE · JACKIE GLEASON
JANE WYMAN
"HOW TO COMMIT MARRIAGE"
TECHNICOLOR®
CRC [M]

Bob and old friend Jane Wyman in How to Commit Marriage *(1969)*

boy grown older. With Fred Clark, Rosemary Clooney, Arlene Dahl, William Demarest, Tony Martin, Millard Mitchell and Robert Strauss. Directed by Claude Binyon. Written by Edmund Hartman and Hal Kanter. Paramount.

48. *Scared Stiff* (1953). Unbilled cameo in the Dean Martin–Jerry Lewis remake of *The Ghostbreakers*.

49. *Casanova's Big Night* (1954). As the tailor's apprentice, Pippo Poppolino, in Venice. With John Carradine, Audrey Dalton, Hope Emerson, Joan Fontaine, Arnold Moss and Basil Rathbone. Directed by Norman Z. McLeod. Written by Edmund Hartmann and Hal Kanter. Paramount.

50. *The Seven Little Foys* (1955). Hope acting seriously as Eddie Foy, vaudeville star. With Jimmy Baird, Linda Bennett, James Cagney, Angela Clarke, Billy Gray, Lydia Reed, Richard Shannon, George Tobias and Milly Vitale. Directed by Melville Shavelson. Written by Jack Rose and Melville Shavelson. Paramount.

51. *That Certain Feeling* (1956). As cartoonist Francis X. Digman in love. With Pearl Bailey, Al Capp, Florenz Ames, David Lewis, Jerry Mathers, Eva Marie Saint and George Sanders. Directed by Norman Panama. Written by William Altman, I. A. L. Diamond, Melvin Frank and Norman Panama. Paramount.

52. *The Iron Petticoat* (1956). As Chuck Lockwood, Air Force officer in the cold war with Russia. With Alexander Gauge, Alan Gifford, Robert Helpmann, Katharine Hepburn, James Robertson Justice, David Kossoff and Noelle Middleton. Directed by Ralph Thomas. Written by Ben Hecht, who later disowns the final version of his effort. MGM.

53. *Beau James* (1957). Hope's second serious role: this time he's New York mayor Jimmy Walker. With Walter Catlett, Paul Douglas, Jimmy Durante (as himself), Joseph Mantell, Darren McGavin, Vera Miles and Alexis Smith. Directed by Melville Shavelson. Written by Jack Rose and Melville Shavelson from the Gene Fowler biography, *Beau James*. Paramount.

54. *Paris Holiday* (1958). A movie star in Paris on a vacation. With Anita Ekberg, Fernandel, Alan Gifford, Martha Hyer, Andre Morell and Preston Sturges. Directed by Gerd Oswald. Written by Edmund Beloin and Dean Riesner. United Artists.

55. *Showdown at Ulcer Gulch* (1958). Promo film made for the *Saturday Evening Post*. With Edie Adams, Orson Bean, Salome Jens, Ernie Kovacs, Chico Marx and Groucho Marx.

Two top comics, Jackie Gleason and Ski Nose, in How to Commit Marriage

56. *Five Pennies* (1959). Cameo as himself in a story about jazz musician Red Nichols. Paramount.

57. *Alias Jesse James* (1959). As Milford Farnsworth selling life insurance in the old West. With Wendell Corey, Jim Davis, Rhonda Fleming, Gloria Talbot, Will Wright and Mary Young. As guest stars James Arness, Ward Bond, Gary Cooper, Bing Crosby, Gail Davis, Hugh O'Brian, Fess Parker, Roy Rogers and Jay Silverheels (Tonto). Directed by Norman McLeod. Written by Daniel D. Beauchamp and William Bowers. Hope–United Artists.

58. *The Facts of Life* (1960). As the man around the house. With Lucille Ball, Louise Beavers, Don De Fore, Ruth Hussey, Peter Leeds, Mike Mazurki, Louis Nye, Philip Ober, Robert F. Simon and Marianne Stewart. Directed by Melvin Frank. Written by Melvin Frank and Norman Panama. United Artists.

59. *Bachelor in Paradise* (1961). As a writer, single, in the suburbs. With Virginia Grey, Jim Hutton, John McGiver, Janis Paige, Don Porter, Paula Prentiss, Clinton Sundberg, Florence Sundstrom and Lana Turner. Directed by Jack Arnold. Written by Walentine Davies and Hal Kanter. MGM.

60. *The Road to Hong Kong* (1962). Last *Road* movie; it plays tired. With Joan Collins, Bing Crosby, Dorothy Lamour and Robert Morley. As guest stars Jerry Colonna, Zsa Zsa Gabor, Dave King, Dean Martin, David Niven, Peter Sellers and Frank Sinatra. Directed by Norman Panama. Written by Melvin Frank and Norman Panama. Melnor–United Artists.

61. *Critic's Choice* (1963). As a sage on the aisle, Parker Ballentine. With Stanley Adams, Lucille Ball, Jim Backus, Jerome Cowan, Dorothy Green, Rick Kellman, Royce Landis, Marilyn Maxwell, Rip Torn, Lurene Tuttle and Marie Windsor. Directed by Don Weis. Written by Jack Sher from the Ira Levin play. Warner Bros.

62. *Call Me Bwana* (1963). As a writer on Africa in Africa. With Edie Adams, Anita Ekberg, Lionel Jeffries and Percy Herbert. Directed by Gordon Douglas. Written by Johanna Harwood and Nate Monaster. Eon–United Artists.

63. *The Sound of Laughter* (1963). Documentary on comedy in early films. Clip of Hope and Leah Ray singing a love duet from *Going Spanish*. Union Film Release.

64. *A Global Affair* (1964). Preserving and protecting women's rights at the United Nations. With Elga Andersen, Michele Mercier

and Lilo Pulver. Directed by Jack Arnold. Written by Bob Fisher, Charles Lederer and Arthur Marx. MGM.

65. *I'll Take Sweden* (1965). Domestic comedy in the land of the midnight sun. With Frankie Avalon, Rosemarie Brankland, Dina Merrill, Jeremy Slate and Tuesday Weld. Directed by Frederick de Cordova. Written by Bob Fisher, Arthur Marx and Nat Perrin. United Artists.

66. *The Oscar* (1966). One scene as the emcee at the Academy Awards. Embassy.

67. *Boy, Did I Get a Wrong Number* (1966). The old marriage mix-up plot for laughs. With Benny Baker, Terry Burnham, Cesare Danova, Phyllis Diller, Joyce Jameson, Marjorie Lord, Elke Sommer, Kelly Thordsen, and Harry Von Zell. Directed by George Marshall. Written by George Kennett, Albert E. Lewin and Burt Styler. United Artists.

68. *Eight on the Lam* (1967). As widower dad, on the run with his brood of seven. With Kevin Brody, Phyllis Diller, Shirley Eaton, Michael Freeman, Bob Fisher, Glenn Gilger, Avis and Robert Hope (Hope's grandchildren), Peter Leeds, Stacey Maxwell, Jill St. John, Debi Storm, Austin Willis and Jonathan Winters. Directed by George Marshall. Written by Bob Fisher, Albert E. Lewin, Arthur Marx and Burt Styler. United Artists.

69. *The Private Navy of Sgt. O'Farrell* (1968). Replay of World War II for grins. With Mylene Demongeot, Phyllis Diller, Jeffrey Hunter, Gina Lollobrigida, William Wellman, Jr. and Henry Wilcoxon. Directed by Frank Tashlin. Written by Frank Tashlin. United Artists.

70. *How to Commit Marriage* (1969). Bliss and banter over the generation gap. With Maureen Arthur, Irwin Corey, Jackie Gleason, Tina Louise, Leslie Nielsen, Paul Stewart and Jane Wyman. Directed by Norman Panama. Written by Michael Kanin and Ben Starr. Cinerama Releasing.

71. *Cancel My Reservation* (1972). As talk-show personality trying to patch up his marriage and fast-talk his way out of a murder rap in Arizona in quick step. With Anne Archer, Ralph Bellamy, Henry Darrow, Chief Dan George, Eva Marie Saint, Forrest Tucker and Keenan Wynn. Directed by Paul Bogart. Written by Robert Fisher and Arthur Marx. Warner Bros.

TELEVISION

Radio made Hope a star. But it was television that made him a superstar and a welcome guest in every American living room. Television enabled Hope to continue basking in the limelight long after his radio career had faded and his Hollywood days as a top box-office draw had ended.

Hope's television career contrasts sharply with those of many of his colleagues in comedy. For twenty-two years Hope has been an NBC network headliner. He has watched all the other big names rise and fall, come and go. Stars of the first magnitude, such as Milton Berle, once dubbed "Mr. Television," George Gobel, Sid Caesar, Red Buttons and Red Skelton, to name just a few, all were comedians with loads of talent who proved their popularity week after week on their regular comedy shows. But somehow they faded away. Hope has outlasted them all.

From the outset, Hope avoided becoming anchored to the grind of a weekly show. Through artful scheduling, his appearances were limited to a maximum of nine shows a season. This decision to avoid overexposure served to enhance his appeal, and no doubt has been a prime factor in his remarkable longevity.

Though a current NBC executive maintains that the network always considered Hope too valuable a property to be wasted on a regular basis, it was, in fact, Hope's incredibly hectic schedule that precluded any attempts to pin him down to a weekly stint.

Hope had flirted with the new entertainment medium on several occasions before 1950. In the early thirties, he teamed with Lulu McConnell and Willie Howard for an experimental show that had been put together by CBS. After a lengthy interval, he appeared in January, 1947, on the first commercial television broadcast in the West.

For that date, he opened the show with his reliable and successful rapid-fire monologue:

This is Bob "First Commercial Television Broadcast" Hope, telling you gals who have tuned me in ... and I wanna make this emphatic ... If my face isn't handsome and debonaire ... It isn't me ... It's the static ... Well, here I am on the air for Lincoln automobiles ... but I find television's a little different than radio ... When I went on the air for Elgin, they gave me a watch ... When I went on the air for Silver Theatre, they gave me a set of Silver ... tonight I'm on for Lincoln ... and they gave me this ... (*holds up a Lincoln penny*) ... If you don't get it, don't knock it ... this is an experimental program! ... (*points to a car*) ... You know, I can remember when they used to drive those things ... my mother used to hold me up to the window to watch 'em go by ... 1911 ... I'm sure of the date because that was the first year that Crosby sang "White Christmas" ... I remember there was one kid in town who used to go down to the junkpile ... get a washboiler, a few wheels, light a smudge fire inside it ... and then try to sell it as a genuine Stanley Steamer ... I wonder what ever became of little Madman Muntz? ... I remember when I got my first car ... I parked so much, I had mohair spread ... what a car ... It could stop on a dime ... it had to ... it couldn't get over it ... It had six cylinders ... two worked ... two didn't ... and the other two just stood around and watched ... That certainly was a long time ago. It seems only yesterday that people were standing around saying Bob Hope was a no good bum who'd never amount to anything in this world ... in fact, it was yesterday, in Henry Ginsberg's office ... but just think ... Here it is 1947 ... and we're holding the first commercial television broadcast in the West ... Commercial ... what a lovely word! ... up 'til tonight, I looked on television as something I might dabble in for a night or so ... A week ... maybe a month ... but now that it's gone commercial ... meet "the yearling!" ... everybody wants me to go into television ... I know they do ... any time I hear somebody discuss my radio program, they always say, "I never could see that guy." ... we're using scripts tonight, but I understand in the future, all the material will have to be learned by heart ... can you imagine? Comedians memorizing their own material? ... incidentally, I'm not allowed to mention my own product tonight ... I had to promise I wouldn't even whisper it ... but I just happen to have with me (*takes huge carton out from under his coat with "Pepsodent" written on it in block letters, holds it up in front of camera, then says to cameraman*) ... bring that thing in a little closer ... some of my listeners may be near-sighted ... (*camera zooms in, he cracks to cameraman*) ... what do you see inside that thing? "Ladies night in a turkish bath?" ... (*to audience*)

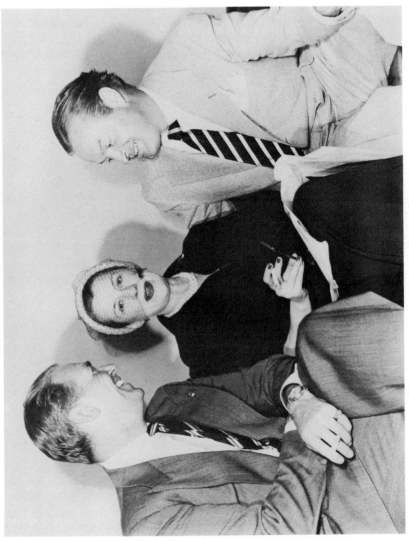

Two of Bob's first TV guest stars, Doug Fairbanks, Jr., and Bea Lillie; third (not pictured) was Dinah Shore

... I know he can't be looking at me ... but, seriously, one thing I love about television is that everyone says it's going to bring back the type of entertainment we used to call "vaudeville" ... and this way, it's much safer ... Ah, vaudeville ... what memories ... gee, the first time I ever appeared on the vaudeville stage, I had a lump in my throat ... A tomato got stuck ... by the time I finished the second show I was paying the spotlight man five bucks to keep me out of it ... Yessir, things weren't always easy ... I used to be a starving actor ... then one day I got a break ... My landlady started putting real cheese in the traps ... I never could afford a press agent ... I had to get all my free advertising by myself ... In fact, I was the Kilroy of my generation ... but I really love the stage ... why, if I had to work for nothing, I'd quit tomorrow ... and so, tonight I think it's appropriate that we run this clambake like the old days of the Orpheum Circuit ... A real vaudeville show ... in the hope that television will be as fine a training ground for new talent as the five-a-day was for all of us ... so, on with the show! Hit, professor! ... (*pause*) ... where's the orchestra? ... (*looks around—a man runs onstage, carrying a small portable phonograph, which he hands to Hope, then exits*) ... Thank you, Mr. Petrillo! ... (*switches phonograph on; as the music starts, camera picks up vaudeville placard reading, "The Rhythmairs"*) ... heading the bill tonight ... the Rhythmairs!

Late in 1949 Hope made a surprise appearance on Ed Sullivan's show, "Toast of the Town." Hope jokingly recalls that he did the show "for nothing."

"Ed was on television two years before it started. He asked me to come over and I went and did an eight-minute monologue just to try out the medium," Hope later remembered in jest.

Hope liked what he tried and began considering the idea of working in the new medium on a steadier basis. Paramount at first was opposed to his appearing on television in his own show because the movie firm was fearful of the dangers of overexposure. But after a bit of friendly persuasion, Paramount changed its mind.

Hope's formal television debut in his own NBC network show was sponsored by Frigidaire. The show was a spectacular musical revue unique for its time, but it was the contract for the show that shattered all precedents. Hope was paid $40,000 for the broadcast, which was aired on April 9, 1950, Easter Sunday. Hope's pay reportedly was four times the highest amount ever paid to a TV single. The total budget for the talent alone exceeded $125,000. By comparison, the entire production budget for each "Milton Berle Hour" that 1950 season totaled $30,000. The "Studio One" dramatic

Bob and Jack Benny in a skit from one of his TV shows

hour presented one show on a budget of $11,000.

The first special was entitled, "Star Spangled Revue." Heading a glittering guest-list of stars were dashing Douglas Fairbanks, Jr., thoroughly British Beatrice Lillie and drawling Dinah Shore. They were backed by a high-stepping chorus of 75 dancers.

The producer was Max Liebman, at the time quite busy also producing Sid Caesar's weekly comedy classic, "Your Show of Shows." This first show set the pattern for all the Hope specials that followed, establishing the practice of inviting only the very top names of the day, and utilizing the musical-comedy show format with a monologue followed by skits, sketches and songs.

After the monologue and a couple of lighthearted skits, Hope and Miss Shore sang and danced in a cute version of "Baby It's Cold Outside." Then came a sketch with Hope, Fairbanks and Miss Lillie. Miss Lillie, an institution in London music hall comedy, followed with a solo gag routine in her incomparable style of sardonic understatement.

But the funniest skit by far in the initial show was a wild distortion of the signing of Hope's first television contract. The set depicted a plush NBC executive suite. Without letup Hope mocked himself, the rivalry between NBC and CBS and comedian Jack Benny. After each mention of CBS, a flurry of junior executives appeared. In a pantomime of fumigation, they scampered about the suite spraying the air with flit-gunned fury. At one point the camera zeroed in on a portrait of Jack Benny veiled by a black mourning drape. At the time Benny was reportedly being wooed by CBS.

Hope's Frigidaire contract called for four more specials. His next outing was broadcast on Mother's Day. His first show had been met by a mixed greeting from the critics, and a reference to the lukewarm reception was included in the monologue.

"How do you do, ladies and gentlemen ... I'm very happy to be here once again on television. This is my second show for the Frigidaire people. I'm surprised too ... " was Hope's impish reply.

In a direct dig at those critics who had written that the first show was disappointing, Hope obliquely implied that they had been unfairly biased and that he was the people's choice.

"I want to thank the thousands of people who wrote letters about the first show ... Also the three who mailed them ... No, I did get about five thousand letters," Hope asserted.

But then he quickly pulled in his horns by joking: "The FBI's going over them now."

Bob Hope and his leading ladies, joined in a reunion on the "Bob Hope Comedy Special" on Wednesday, September 28, 1966. The beauties surrounding Hope are: (front row) Lucille Ball (Sorrowful Jones, 1948; Fancy Pants, 1949; Facts of Life, 1960. Critic's Choice, 1962); Joan Fontaine (Casanova's Big Night, 1953); Hedy Lamarr (My Favorite Spy, 1951); Signe Hasso (Where There's Life, 1946); (Back row) Joan Collins (Road to Hong Kong, 1962); Virginia Mayo (Princess and the Pirate, 1944); Vera Miles (Beau James, 1956); Janis Paige (Bachelor in Paradise, 1961)—and, of course, Dorothy Lamour

The rest of the monologue was vintage Hope, mocking others with a light touch and himself with a heavier hand.

"It's amazing how many people see you on TV. I did my first television show a month ago and the next day five million television sets were sold. The people who couldn't sell theirs threw them away," he cracked. The approach was impossible to resist. He never seemed to take himself seriously, and he definitely was not a prima donna.

After his second show the critics were gentler. Part of the reason may have been two of his guests, two singers named Frank Sinatra and Peggy Lee.

Several explanations have been advanced regarding Hope's early difficulties in mastering the intricate performing demands of television. One very close to home was offered by his wife Dolores, who once confided:

> Of course in the beginning, on television, Bob was experimenting. He was too aware of the visual, he was trying to find what audiences would laugh to *see*. Well, there's no question about it, if someone throws a custard pie at Bob the audience will laugh; but anyone can be hit in the face with a pie. They'll laugh much longer (years longer) over a light comedy situation, which is Bob's forte and which makes him unique. He knows that now. He knows that he doesn't have to be the one to wear the funny shoes and the comic hat. His new shows ... show you what I mean and they show a good deal more rehearsal too; and instead of a strained effort—his incomparable ease.

Hope himself once was asked if he was frightened by television. He replied:

> Not any more. I think I've got hold of it now. In the beginning it was a real problem for me because of the television studios. Every time I'd be ready to let loose with a gag, a guy with earphones would walk by pointing at me and waving his arms. It was like trying to do a nightclub show with three waiters, with trays, walking in front of you every time you reached the punch line.
>
> Television technicians are murder for a comedian. I finally reached the solution. I tied down the cameras and gave orders that no one moves while the show is on. From there on out it was clear sailing. The only way not to get killed on television is to set it up the way you want it, not the way they want it.

Hope managed to solve his dilemma only after much thought and considerable self-analysis. He mistakingly had carried over into television the highpowered broadcasting techniques he had learned

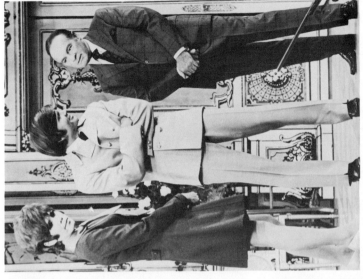

*(Left) Janis Paige and Bob in a scene from the 1969 TV revival of Roberta
(Right) Michele Lee, John Davidson and Bob in the same show*

193

in radio. However, because the TV camera lens acted as a magnifying glass, performing on television demanded a much more subdued pace. In the living room on the picture tube, each gesture and each joke instantly was blown up many times its actual studio lifesize. So, after an agonizing start, Hope discovered the secret. Thereafter, he played everything down-tempo.

Years later, Hope discussed his attempt to conquer television. He wrote:

> I honestly think that the secret of TV is being relaxed, casual and easy. I used to work very fast on radio because I found out when I was working for service audiences that they wanted it fast. They didn't want situation comedy; they wanted jokes and they wanted them right now; they wanted them to go bang, bang, bang. I was successful with them that way. I carried this technique over into my first days on television, but it wasn't too successful. With that particular type of material and a civilian audience, I was ahead of them, and working too fast for them. I've slowed down for television, especially with my monologue.
>
> The truth is that when you're right in the room with those who watch you and listen to you, as you are in TV, practically sitting in their laps and muttering into their ears, your personality is more important than anything you can say. If you say something with a little hook—you're home because it's the personality which counts. What I'm trying to put across is, whatever you say on TV, it's as much the *way* you say it as *what* you say.

Although Hope eventually mastered the medium, he has never managed to overcome the consistent hostility of the metropolitan critics who write about it. Particular specials have been hailed on occasion, but most of Hope's shows have been panned (including the first full-hour commercial show on color television back in 1953).

However, unlike many of his counterparts, who won terrific notices only to get bogged down in rating problems, Hope year after year continues to notch a spot near or at the top of the heap each season. His Christmas shows in 1970 and 1971 reportedly scored the highest Nielsen ratings ever for specials.

His opening show for the 1972 season ranked second only to the phenomenally successful first-run presentation of the 1971 smash film hit, *Love Story*. His popularity is also broadly based. An analysis of the demographic Nielsens revealed that Hope scored in the top ten for all age groups except teens (12–17) and children (2–11).

Numbers like these make a favorable impression on prospective sponsors. Thus, Hope has never encountered problems lining up

(Above) Michelle Lee and Bob in a scene from his TV revival of Roberta in 1969
(Below) Janis Paige and Bob in a scene from the same TV show

companies willing to underwrite the escalating costs of his shows (currently, the cost of airing a Hope special is reportedly in the area of $1 million).

But the Hope-sponsor relationship has not been entirely blissful. There have been spats, some nasty, in both radio and television. In one memorable clash, a sponsor became enraged when Hope ignored a warning and appeared on a Frank Sinatra special a few years ago. Hope was dropped immediately. Unshaken by the sudden blast, he quickly found another angel.

Sponsors find the high ratings irresistible, but Hope appeals to sponsors for another significant reason. They know he not only performs, he also participates in the overall presentation of their product to the public. As Sid Eigis, NBC vice president in charge of public information, explained: "Hope gives a lot of extra value for his money."

Part of that added value includes Hope's continuing practice of stressing sponsor identification, a holdover from his radio days. Hope's shows always have incorporated the sponsor's name in the title—"The Bob Hope Chrysler Show," to cite a recent example. Though he himself does not deliver the commercials, Hope becomes involved with other sales activities. For instance, it's not unusual for him to appear at major sales conventions or similar company functions. On his public appearance dates at state fairs and colleges, Hope often refers to his current sponsor in his gags.

Hope considers these offscreen efforts as vital to the promotion of his shows and his career. He once explained: "I think sponsor identification is very important but it's got to be subtle, and worked in so it doesn't seem like you're pressing."

He views the product, the show and himself as a single property which is supposed to be promoted vigorously. "If my ratings are high it's partly due to the fact that when I do my TV shows, I'm doing a spectacular each time I come busting out of the starting gate ... as far as exploitation and promotion are concerned, I have to treat each one as if it's a spectacular. If I don't I'm dead. A guy in my business should know that," he noted.

Hope further clarified his approach by adding: "It's getting out there in person and selling each show like there's not going to be any tomorrow. I get behind every show I'm in and push it as if it's a new musical comedy or a new feature length movie. I try to steam people up about my name all over again."

About a week or two before the scheduled broadcast of a Hope

Bob advising Michelle Lee how to get the man she loves in the TV revival of
Roberta in 1969

television special, there's a hectic scramble of carefully planned publicity activity. It's not unusual to see him make guest appearances on the top talk shows, in addition to sitting down to a host of interviews with newspaper and magazine feature writers. His New York–based public relations firm, the Kalmus Corporation, and the NBC publicity department distribute slickly written and comprehensive press data in attractive kits to newspaper offices across the country.

According to Hope himself, the publicity efforts do not end at that point. At times they continue in a personal way. He explains: "Another thing I do, I put in long distance calls for people who write about TV shows and TV personalities. For instance, I call the guy who writes up TV for the Roanoke, Virginia paper and I'll say, 'Hi! This is Bob Hope.'"

The star-studded format of Hope's shows has always provided a natural and valuable source of promotional copy. The comedian has never varied his practice of booking top show business stars, or names currently at the top of the news no matter what their field. Some of his most famous guests have included Milton Berle, Bing Crosby, Sammy Davis, Jr., Juliet Prowse, Jimmy Durante, Jack Jones, Phyllis Diller, Tom Jones, Raquel Welch and Ray Bolger. Also, Eva Gabor, Ingrid Bergman, Lucille Ball, Danny Thomas, Joan Crawford and George Burns.

Big names in the headlines of the day have included Don Larsen, Yankee pitcher and baseball hero, who in 1956 hurled the only perfect World Series game, and Diana Dors, a well-built blonde British movie actress whose well-publicized fall offscreen into a pool at a wild Hollywood party made international news. More recently, Olympic swimming legend Mark Spitz, the only man in history to win seven gold medals, and the 1972 World Champion of Chess, Bobby Fisher, were Hope guests.

Spitz and Fisher appeared on the same show, and Hope made it a specific point to personally thank both men for their heroic efforts in the field of international competition. Hope also expressed gratitude to them on behalf of the American people.

The script usually capitalizes on the event that catapulted the guest into the headlines. In a skit with chess champ Fisher, most of the gags related to his fabled ego and his fearsome reputation for crushing an opponent's will and self-esteem. Pointed references also were made to Fisher's bizarre showdown in Iceland with Russian chess czar Boris Spassky, who was dethroned as world chess king by

Bob and Phyllis Diller in a scene from a 1968 telecast

the cocky Fisher in the most publicized chess match in history.

As the following excerpt from a 1956 show reveals, Hope had a ball with Diana Dors in a skit that capitalized on her infamous pool plunge to the top of the news:

Hope: Ladies and gentlemen, tonight, we welcome to our stage a young lady who recently made a very big splash in Hollywood. This attractive young actress started at the bottom and swam her way to the top. Here she is ... England's answer to Esther Williams ... Miss Diana Dors! Beautiful, isn't she? No wonder everyone had to jump in the pool. Good evening, Diana.

Dors: Good evening, Sir Robert.

Hope: Please ... not here. It's not necessary.

Dors: But in England you told me you were America's Olivier.

Hope: Well, it's not official yet. Ike hasn't knighted me with his putter. Diana, I'm glad you finally made it to our shores.

Dors: Thanks to you, Bob. After all, you're the one who discovered me in England.

Hope: Well, I can't take too much credit for finding you. It's not exactly like looking for a needle in a haystack. I expected a little more gratitude from you, but the first thing you do when you arrive is run off and make a picture with a total stranger.

Dors: Oh, you mean my new picture with George Gobel. Isn't he adorable, Bob?

Hope: Personally, I find him quite vulgar.

Dors: George? Vulgar?

Hope: Exceedingly. Do you know that he goes around in public saying funny things?

Dors: I found George to be a perfect gentleman. Not once in all the time we were together did he try to kiss me.

Hope: You just weren't around when there was a step ladder handy.

Dors: Bob, you know I'd adore making a picture with you.

Hope: Really.

Dors: Why, it would be the biggest thrill of my life to make a "Road" picture with you and that other fellow ... What's his name?

Hope: I had it on the tip of my tongue, but I spit it out.

Dors: Well, he's nice, Bob ... but after all, you're the one that's the big attraction.

Hope: Me? Where'd you get that idea?

Dors: It says so right on the card.

Hope: Please ... don't destroy the illusion. Di, I know this is your

Phyllis Diller and Bob in a skit from a 1968 telecast

first visit here ... how do the colonies strike you?

Dors: Oh, they're cute.

Hope: Well, good night everybody in Texas. You flew over the country, didn't you?

Dors: Uh huh.

Hope: Well, this may come as a surprise to you, but as the plane gets closer to the ground, the states get bigger.

Dors: Bob, you don't have to explain things like that to me. I'm not exactly ... what would you Americans say ... a square?

Hope: No ... we'd never say that. Incidently, Diana, how are you doing with the language barrier?

Dors: Oh, I love the way you Yanks talk, it's so colorful.

Hope: Like what? What's your favorite expression?

Dors: "Alimony." It has such an intriguing sound. What does it mean?

Hope: They don't have that in England?

Dors: I've never heard it.

Hope: Last one to the boat is a schnook. Well, do you understand the political speeches that Ike and Adlai are making?

Dors: Well, no, but it's all very exciting. Which man do you think will make the best King?

Hope: Either one ... they both have shiny crowns. Diana, it's not King ... it's President.

Dors: I like our system better. A King reigns for his entire life ... except of course for the one who abdicated.

Hope: I remember him. He's the one who ran and married the "jacks" player. Diana, I get the feeling that you prefer England to America.

Dors: England's wonderful ... but for a woman, America is the greatest place in the world. I love the way the American men treat their wives.

Hope: Don't be ridiculous. Men are men ... and women are women all over the world. At the last meeting of the UN even Russia voted for that.

Dors: Bob, you don't understand. In Europe a woman is trained to worship her man. The wife is a slave ... the husband is King.

Hope: Last one to the boat is a schnook.

Many of Hope's television specials are created around a central theme. A frequent topic is Hope's career in vaudeville. In one show, Hope joined with Jack Jones and Jimmy Durante to demonstrate that oldtime hoofing can still be fun. In another show based on

202

Milton Berle, Petula Clark, Sammy Davis, Jr., and Juliet Prowse join Bob in a 1972 show saluting his vaudeville days

Hope's nostalgia for his vaudeville days, the theme saluted the good old days of breaking in a new act out on the road and then bringing it in from the hinterland for a headline shot at the Palace. Guest stars Milton Berle, Juliet Prowse, Sammy Davis, Jr., and Petula Clark joined Hope in a sketch recreating a classic vaudeville routine entitled "School Daze." Petula Clark portrayed the teacher attempting to impart some wisdom to her reluctant charges (Hope and company) and making very little headway.

In another skit Hope recalled the kind of banter he and members of the orchestra traded when he made his debut at the Palace in the thirties. Berle took the part of the annoying violinist. The show also featured Hope and Sammy Davis, Jr., interpreting the old buck and wing, a lively number that took Hope and his viewers back in time to where it all began for him in Cleveland.

Hope frequently used his success in other areas of show business as inspiration for his telecasts. His fondness for his 1933 Broadway show, *Roberta*, prompted him to revive it for television on two different occasions. In 1958 he opened his season with *Roberta*, helped by co-stars Janis Paige, Howard Keel and Anna Maria Alberghetti. A little more than a decade later the show was updated once more. Janis Paige co-starred along with two members of the younger set, Singers John Davidson and Michele Lee. Neither singer had been born when the original run of *Roberta* opened on Broadway. The setting for the plot is a Parisian dress shop. For the 1969 presentation famed Gallic couturier Hubert Givenchy was retained to supply the outfits for a spectacular fashion show.

In 1955 Hope used his motion picture career as the theme for his last show of the season. Helping Hope to reminisce were some of his former leading ladies. The famous faces included Jane Russell, Madeleine Carroll, Dorothy Lamour and Paulette Goddard.

The show also featured film clips from dozens of his films. Included were *Paleface, Son of Paleface, Ghostbreakers, Monsieur Beaucaire, Caught in the Draft, Sorrowful Jones, The Seven Little Foys* and four of the *Road* movies.

Herald Tribune critic John Crosby, who for years somehow managed to hand Hope the worst notices, changed 180 degrees and hailed the program. He wrote in his column:

"I thought it was just great ... For instance, Hope wrestling with that gorilla in the clip from *Road to Bali* is as funny a bit of nonsense as you're likely to see anywhere. The duet between Hope and Bing Crosby "Put It There Pal" was a big hit record of its day. And where

Tom Jones and Bob singing a duet in a 1970 telecast

can you get a lineup of leading ladies like that?"

The show received such a genuinely warm welcome that Hope did a similar show for his September 28 telecast in 1966. He called it "Bob Hope and His Leading Ladies." He invited Lucille Ball, Joan Fontaine, Hedy Lamarr, Signe Hasso, Joan Collins, Virginia Mayo, Vera Miles, Janis Paige and, of course, Dorothy Lamour.

The shows that have been the most outstanding feature of his television career have been his Christmas specials. The first holiday show he ever did on film was his 1954 Yuletide visit to Thule, Greenland, a frigid outpost in the nation's outer air defense network. His guests were William Holden, soon to become an Academy Award winner for his role in *Stalag 17*, Hedda Hopper, Margaret Whiting and Jerry Colonna. Hope also brought along an ice-melter, the sizzling, statuesque winner of the Miss UCLA beauty contest —Anita Ekberg. Until that year her only fans had been college boys. After the show it was every male over 13.

Hope's practice of adapting his monologue to the life and the lot of the troops was a big hit with the GIs and the TV audience at home in the states. At Thule his wit was at its sharpest, darting through the cold, the loneliness and the woman shortage with pinpoint accuracy. His icebreaker at the top of the world began:

> I'm very happy to be here at Thule. The temperature is 36 below. We don't know below what, the thermometer just went over the hill! ... It's really cold here. One guy jumped out of his bunk at 6 A.M. this morning, ran in and turned on the shower, and was stoned to death! ... It was so cold last night, one GI fell out of bed and broke his pajamas! ... Up here, a pin-up calendar isn't a luxury, it's a necessity! We certainly got a wonderful reception when we landed. All those soldiers standing at attention! I understand they've been that way for four months! ... When I walked into General O'Donnell's quarters, the first thing I noticed was the tail of a reindeer sticking out of the wall over the fireplace. I said, "How come you didn't mount the antlers?" He said, "Don't be silly, it's not mounted, that's a live one trying to get warm!"

When the concept of filmed TV shows caught on with the viewing public, Hope began the practice of weaving the shooting schedule for them into his other show business activities. While on location in England to make *The Iron Petticoat* with Katharine Hepburn in 1956, Hope filmed many of the shows he did at American bases ringing London.

Hope's deftness at plugging his sponsor's product at the same time

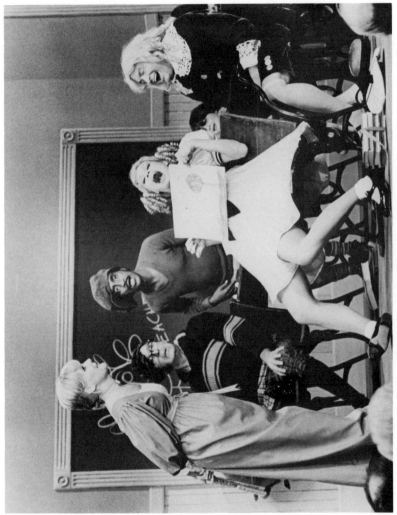

Petula Clark, Milton Berle, Sammy Davis, Jr., Juliet Prowse and Bob recreate the famous "School Daze" sketch from vaudeville

207

he cracks jokes is shown perfectly in this opening line from one of those shows: "You know what a Rolls Royce is—that's a Chevy that's been knighted."

In 1958, Hope used Russian entertainment as the theme for his Easter show. He journeyed to Moscow after a struggle to obtain visas for himself and four of his aides. Endless conferences with Communist officials were held. The show, which was filmed by Soviet camera crews, turned out to be one of Hope's most memorable specials. It became a major news event, and for a time succeeded in heating up the cold war.

Although the Russians expressed an army of reservations over some of the material in the monologue, they proved to be quite cooperative. Finally approved, the jokes caused a major diplomatic flap in the Kremlin because they lampooned aspects of Soviet life considered sacred by many top commissars.

For example:

●The Russians are overjoyed with their Sputnik. It's kind of weird being in a country where every ninety-two minutes there's a national holiday.

●Anybody without a stiff neck is a traitor.

●It's the big topic of conversation every place but the dog show.

The monologue continued in a softer tone and touched on less sensitive topics:

●Surprisingly enough, I'm not having any trouble with the language. Nobody talks to me.

●Russian television viewers are a lot like Americans. They're crazy about Westerns. There's only one difference. They root for the Indians.

The rest of the show consisted of scenes of the Russian entertainment world. The Ukrainian State Dance ensemble was seen performing its incredibly athletic dance routines. Also captured on film were the performing bears of the Moscow Circus, the flowing grace of the Bolshoi's prima ballerina, Galina Ulanova, and a travelogue featuring views of the Kremlin, Red Square and street scenes in snow-bound Moscow.

Hope's TV appearances have not been limited to his own specials. In addition to numerous guest shots, he hosted the weekly dramatic series, "Bob Hope presents the Chrysler Theatre." He did a daily five-minute commentary during the 1952 Republican and Democratic conventions for NBC radio and television. He has hosted a variety of telethons, including one in 1972 to aid victims in the

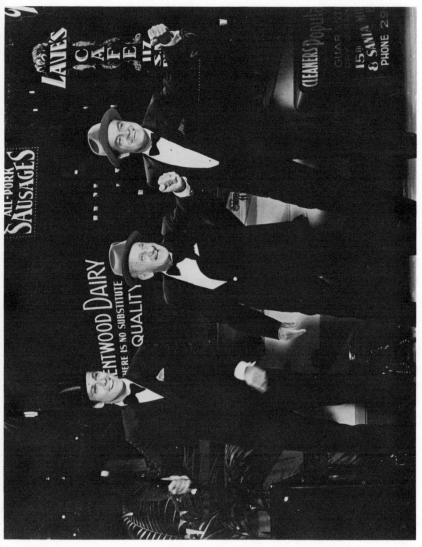

Jack Jones, Jimmy Durante and Bob in a dance routine from one of his TV shows offering a nostalgic look at vaudeville

countryside surrounding flood-ravaged Wilkes Barre, Pa.

Hope has become noted for his role as master of ceremonies of the Academy Awards. Since his first appearance in 1941, Hope has piloted the Oscar derby fourteen times. Not all these shows were telecast, of course, but to millions of viewers Hope and the ceremonial awards show became synonymous.

A veteran Hollywood observer explained: "It's like Jimmy Durante's old song, 'I Can Do without Broadway, but Can Broadway Do without Me?' Hope can do without the Academy but can the Academy do without Hope?"

Since Hope opened his first Oscar night thirty-one years ago with the line, "I'm very happy to be here for my annual insult," he has parlayed his record of never winning an award for his acting into a guaranteed laugh-grabber. In 1953 he joked: "I like to be here in case one of these years they'll have one left over." In 1967: "I don't mind losing, but I hate to go home and explain to my kids how the actors I've been sneering at all year beat me out." In 1968: "Welcome to the Academy Awards—or, as it's known at my house—Passover."

Although Hope has never won an Oscar for any role on the screen, he's been the recipient of honorary awards from the Academy on five occasions. In 1941 he was given a silver plaque and cited "For his unselfish services to the motion picture industry." In 1945 he won life membership in the Academy. In 1954 he was awarded an honorary Oscar for "his contribution to the laughter of the world, his services to the motion picture industry and his devotion to the American premise." In 1961 he was presented with the Jean Hersholt Humanitarian Award "for outstanding service to his fellow man" and in 1966 he was awarded a gold medal for "unique and distinctive service to the academy and the industry." Hope had been presented with an Oscar in 1946 as a joke. It was one inch tall.

Hope's emcee role has almost always received warm praise from the critics. His handling of the prestigious ceremony has always been deft, and his casual attitude and refreshing quips usually provide a timely breather between the pretentious and sentimental acceptance speeches.

The Emmy has also given Hope the cold shoulder. In twenty-two years of telecasting, he has never been named best comedian. He has not been shut out, however. In 1966 his Christmas show was awarded the Emmy for being the outstanding variety special of that

Bing and Bob do a buck and wing dance on the telecast of the opening of Madison Square Garden in 1968

year. In 1959 he was the recipient of the annual Trustee Award "for bringing the great gift of laughter to all peoples of all nations."

Bob and Crosby in a Christmas skit on TV

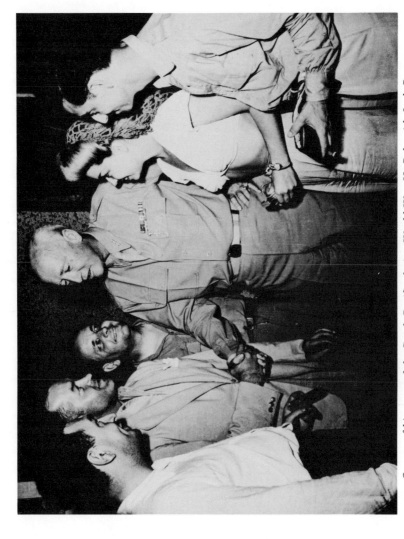

On one of his tours of the South Pacific during World War II, Bob, with Jack Pepper, Frances Langford and Tony Romano, meets Admiral Nimitz

USO TOURS

Hope shambles out onstage at the army gym (doo-de-doo-de-doo-de-doo) just doing Hope, you know, joking around, and he's wearing, dig, these knee-length Bavarian lederhosen, a German Mao jacket, and some absurd Tyrolian hat with one of those goofy brushes stuck in it—a walking sight gag. And a roar starts to well up from the 5,000 troops out there, but he just keeps shucking around the stage, oblivious, swinging that three-wood he always carries, and that's all it takes. The house collapses.
The Overseas Weekly—Pacific Edition, Saturday, Jan. 16, 1971

By the time World War II began, Hope was a star. In those years and in those times, patriotism was a strong belief in the rectitude of the American way and an almost consuming regard for the well-being and morale of "our boys"—the airdales, dogfaces, gobs and jarheads.

That once fairly common feeling lies at the heart of the most unique and at times most controversial aspect of Hope's tenure as America's top comedian—his efforts on behalf of American servicemen.

Unique because Bob was once dubbed by *Variety*, the show business newspaper, as "America's No. 1 Soldier in Greasepaint."

Controversial because of the maddening complexity of the Vietnam War, which led a firmly entrenched incumbent president, Lyndon Johnson, to decide not to run again, and which divided a troubled nation into two angry and hostile camps—hawks and doves.

Bob Hope has been the laugh mascot for America's men at arms for twenty-nine years. The magnitude of his achievements in this affair of mutual regard is unparalleled in the annals of that sometimes tough and cynical racket called show business.

Hope has flown, sailed, driven and walked millions of miles to be with the troops. In conditions that ranged from mostly uncomfortable to uncomfortably hazardous, the Hope wit has wisecracked to GI's in Berlin, the Pacific, England, Iceland, Alaska, Europe, the Orient, West Germany, the Caribbean, "Gitmo"—Guantanamo Bay in Fidel Castro's Cuba, Newfoundland, Greenland, North Africa, Korea, Guam, the Philippines and, more recently, Thailand and South Vietnam.

But it was because of his annual tours to Southeast Asia—a total of nine—that Hope found himself entangled in a swirl of controversy. Times and attitudes were changing and he was having a difficult time changing with them, because, mainly, they went against his righteously patriotic grain.

His brand of patriotism was expressed in the phrase "America, right or wrong." But many in America's younger set, and more than a few senior citizens, viewing the concept of patriotism from a slightly different, slightly sophisticated and, critics charged, slightly subversive perspective, read the phrase as "America right and wrong."

To Hope's surprise, the Vietnam War rapidly became the symbol of this philosophical difference.

The youth of America was not the only segment of our society to become politicalized by the war. Hollywood, Broadway and the world of entertainment between joined the fray.

Suddenly, performers didn't want to pursue their aspirations of success in front of the troops who were fighting the war no one seemed to want to win. Vietnam had laid an egg.

But it didn't happen overnight. During the first few years of the war in the mid-60's, stars responded as they had during World War II and the conflict in Korea.

But as the furor over the morality of Vietnam heated to a tumult, some entertainers' desire to meet the troops overseas became less than ardent.

It wasn't anything definite, but beginning about 1966 USO officials became increasingly vexed by the growing number of show business figures who seemed to be working elsewhere.

Skeptical officials began to wonder how so many show careers could possibly blossom at the same time, tying entertainers down to "other dates."

When approached by USO booking agents, more and more show figures pleaded lack of time because of prior or pressing engagements.

216

Dottie Lamour and Bob arriving at March Field in 1941 for his first GI show

Bob and a GI

A few years ago Samuel Anderson, executive director of the USO, was quoted as saying in his Saigon office that he felt some personalities, because the war had become so unpopular back home, didn't want to risk becoming identified with it.

Theorized Anderson: "There's been nothing official that we've run into about people being reluctant to come to Vietnam. But the attitude many Americans have about this war apparently has carried over into the entertainment industry."

That attitude did not carry over to Bob Hope, Martha Raye, George Jessel, Raymond Burr or Sebastian Cabot.

The biggest star, Hope, was also the biggest exception.

He refused to abandon his annual USO Christmas tours, and he also remained outspoken in his support of the military:

"Everybody I talked to there wants to know why they can't go in and finish it, and don't let anybody kid you about why we're there. If we weren't, those Commies would have the whole thing, and it wouldn't be long until we'd be looking at them off the coast of Santa Monica."

An ardent anti-Communist, he supported both the Republican administration of President Richard Nixon and the contention that the South Vietnamese people wanted and needed our nation's help in their fight to preserve their tiny nation's sovereignty.

His frank criticism of the ideological tenets of the left, coupled with his well-publicized friendship with Vice President Spiro Agnew, who had become America's sharpest hawk, transformed Hope into a prime target of abuse from American doves.

Never one for a display of public rancor, Hope nonetheless was marked by some of the incidents that occurred during this time, which grew out of his unwanted image as the symbol of America's presence in war-weary Southeast Asia.

For example, in 1971 the New York City Council of Churches voted to present him with their Family of Man Award.

Amid a howl of protest from a group of young activist clergymen, critical of Hope's support of the way the war was being waged by the military and political establishment, the council withdrew the award.

The comedian's reaction was carefully measured.

"I'm not in favor of any war, but I'm also not in favor of surrender," Hope told newsmen.

"This is a touchy conflict. We're helping people maintain their freedom ... I'm not a hawk. I'm an owl," he explained.

He further defined his brand of patriotism by saying: "I appreciate the Americans who have laid down their lives for our country. I get hooked on that kind of thing, and if that stops me from getting awards then I'll have to live with it."

It was ironic that Hope found himself the target of antiwar activists since few have spoken as eloquently as he about the horrors of war.

In his book *I Never Left Home*, published in 1944, Hope wrote:

I saw your sons and your husbands, your brothers and your sweethearts. I saw how they worked, played, fought, and lived. I saw some of them die. I saw more courage, more good humor in the face of discomfort, more love in an era of hate, and more devotion to duty than could exist under tyranny.

And I came back to find people exulting over the thousand plane raids over Germany ... and saying how wonderful they are. Those people never watched the face of a pilot as he read a bulletin board and saw his buddy marked up missing. Those thousand plane raids are wonderful only because of the courage and spirit of the men who make them possible.

We at home would understand all this better if every one of us could go through a few hospital wards, stop at a few emergency dressing stations, pray for our own courage in operating rooms as we watched twelve and eighteen teams of steel-fingered surgeons perform miracles of science on men who had performed miracles of courage.

During the Vietnam conflict, Hope developed a special personal concern for those men at arms captured by the North Vietnamese and jailed in bamboo prisons in combat areas or in internment camps surrounding Hanoi.

In Christmas, 1971, he visited North Vietnamese Communist officials in Laos and offered them $10 million to be turned over to children's charities in return for the immediate release of all POW's. The offer was made to Nguyen Van Thanh, first secretary of the North Vietnamese Embassy in Vientiane.

Hope also requested permission to visit and entertain the captured troops. Both requests were denied by officials in Hanoi.

A tireless showman onstage for the troops on duty in the field, he also has been a quiet Samaritan to the troops on the mend in aid stations and hospitals.

While he cracks jokes such as, "Did you see our show or were you sick before?" to the wounded, his aides are busy taking down the names and addresses of the ward patients.

A lesser known aspect of Hope's kinship with the troops is his practice of sending a letter to each wounded man's family, enclosing a picture of himself with *his arms around* a husband, a father, a son or a brother.

Hope's career as a GI entertainer began three decades ago. His first troop show was at the Army Air Force base at March Field, California in 1941. World War II was raging in Europe but without the active participation of the United States. However, the military was beginning to train seriously for what fate had deemed inevitable.

During the next year and a half Hope remained stateside with the bulk of the troops, visiting training installations and bases at various domestic locations.

His globetrotting began in 1942, some months after the Congress had granted President Franklin D. Roosevelt's request for a declaration of war against Japan and the Axis powers.

Throughout the war, and, in fact, until 1948, Hope's main troop shows were also used for his radio programs—some 400 of these were broadcast.

There were hundreds of others not on the list of 400. These included three or four shows daily at the numerous bases and the weekly shows performed for airing over the Armed Services Radio Service under such titles as "Command Performance," "Male Call" and "GI Journal."

Hope's talent for quips about the remoteness of base locations and the double-standard class system of service life made him an instant hit with the enlisted ranks. The Willies and Joes, later etched graphically by cartoonist Bill Mauldin, loved him the minute he walked onstage, if only because of their gratitude for his biting satire on the grand scale of living of the officer corps.

Hope's early trademark of identifying with the enlisted man and with his gripes about his life and his lot rapidly changed him from a visitor to a buddy. In time the troops accepted him as one of their own who told jokes. He has belonged for over thirty years.

On the air he toned things down a bit, what with the censors and all, but he still made his point, as illustrated in these excerpts from an October, 1944 broadcast:

> This is Bob "back in California and broadcasting from the Navy Ground School at Point Loma" Hope, telling you to use Pepsodent and even if you're just a boot, you won't have to worry about brass when you wanna open your snoot ...
> Well, it's really a pleasure to be back in California ... California

... that's an abbreviation meaning, "Sunshine, orange juice, Hedy Lamarr, and run for high ground every February" ... I spent a few days in Hollywood ... and how that town has changed in the past few weeks ... It's really pitiful to see the civilians following the servicemen down Vine Street hollering, "Come on, drop it, you've smoked it enough" ... Well, here we are at Point Loma. This base is a school for the Navy's signal corps. Isn't that silly? Imagine teaching a sailor how to signal ... and I found out why they call it Point Loma ... I went into the barracks this morning and a sailor asked me, "I just missed my Point ... will you Loma me ten bucks?" ... On the way down I saw a workman at the training station hanging new doors on the barracks ... He said, "I put new doors on this place every six weeks ... It's boot camp, and when the boys graduate, they don't wait to turn the knobs ...

He was still at it a year later, as this excerpt shows:

Well, here I am at Camp Cooke ... Camp Cooke ... this is where they bring guys and let 'em stew for a while before they tell 'em what's on the menu ... I flew up in a Piper Cub ... you know what that is, folks ... aviation's Sinatra ... was that plane small. I opened the cockpit and a sparrow flying overhead dropped in two worms ... it took us a while to make the trip but it wasn't the fault of the plane. All the way up we were battling a bumble bee's backwash ... but it was a lovely trip up. I said to the pilot, "Don't you think we should gain more altitude?" he said, "What for. It's cooler here under the trees." ... They have a lot of sandstorms up here ... I don't know how thick they are ... but when I walked into camp a gopher said, "Hey, buddy, help me outa this tree" ... and it gets very foggy here ... the fog is so low I just saw a private going over to the PX and he was being led by a seeing-eye snake ... these guys [combat vets of the 13th and 20th Armored Divisions awaiting discharge] landed in New York and came out here by troop train ... Troop train ... that's a crap game with a caboose ... I won't say the train was old ... but between Chicago and Kansas City, Jesse James held it up three times ...

These tankmen were very disgusted with the engineer ... every time they went over a deep canyon they'd say, "He must be getting soft ... he's using the bridge" ... and I won't say the train traveled slow but as they were coming into town, a soldier leaned out of the window to whistle at a girl and by the time the train pulled out of the station, he'd met her parents, bought a ring, had a chaplain marry 'em, and was standing on the observation platform waving goodbye to his son.

It hasn't been all laughs and lovely long legs during Bob's

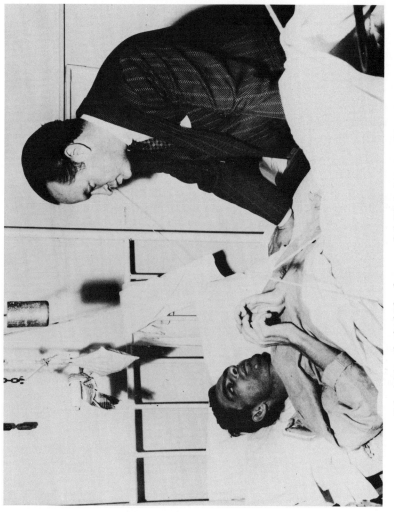

Bob visiting the bedside of a wounded GI during one of his tours

missions of mirth overseas. On occasion only luck kept him from playing heaven.

In Vincenza, Italy, during the 1958 Christmas tour, the troupe was ready to board a plane for a flight to Frankfurt.

Minutes before takeoff, the pilot ordered the fuel checked. His sixth sense averted disaster.

Instead of conventional fuel, a check revealed that JP-5, jet fuel, had been pumped into the tanks. Had the plane gotten off the ground, it probably would have exploded in mid-air.

Despite safety precautions Hope has suffered some injuries while performing for the troops. While on a tour of North Africa in 1943, he hurt his knee.

The area had been hit by a series of air raids. During one raid the comedian sought cover from the bombs by leaping into a ditch. He severely wrenched his knee, and was forced to use a cane for the rest of the tour.

Hope's ability to transcend his superstar status and establish a common feeling with the servicemen is illustrated by the response he received at his first appearance after the injury.

Limping, leaning on the cane for support, dirty and visibly tired, Hope inched to centerstage on a hastily built platform at a racetrack in Bône, Algeria.

His customary, "Good afternoon, everybody," was instantly interrupted with this rough and ready taunt.

"Hi ya, slacker,"shouted a dogface critic sitting down in front. Both the audience and Hope collapsed in laughter.

More than any other star who came to entertain them, Hope belonged. He knew the rules of men at war.

He understood that overt emotion was not wanted. Sympathy expressed openly was for the civilian set. Combat etiquette demanded that it be expressed silently.

The mocking tone was the soldier's way of getting past the moment, getting on with life and around the ever-present possibility of death.

Hope followed this code and played the game accordingly.

Upon entering a ward filled with GI's in traction, he would quip: "Okay fellas. Don't get up."

This banter and his outwardly calm acceptance of their plight helped the wounded to bear their fate with grace.

The makeup of his shows for servicemen has remained basically the same through the years. The major thrust of the show is comedy.

But Hope also has always understood that guys may enjoy other guys telling jokes, but gals dancing, singing or just standing there will be the hit of the show.

So his troupes always have a striking delegation from the fairer sex.

Some doughty critics have opined that the presence of pretty girls is just too tantalizing and exploitative, that all that looking with no chance of touching is a danger to morale.

To this kind of comment, Hope once replied:

> Of course some people don't think the USO should send pretty girls overseas because they get the fellows too excited. I think that's ridiculous. I think the fellows should see what they're fighting for.
>
> I say this because a preacher named Bob Harrington from Bourbon Street in New Orleans recently came back from Vietnam and said we shouldn't send any more sexy girls over there. I just found out the name of his congregation. It's called "Party Poopers."
>
> I don't know why he's complaining. I've been down to Bourbon Street and it's not exactly a boulevard of Phyllis Dillers.
>
> The last guy Phyllis stirred up was Batman. He took one look and flew away.
>
> But I'm glad we have the kind of guys over there who do get excited when they see a pretty girl. It's comforting to know that when the Cong wave a white flag our boys don't wave back. Thank God the only fliers we've got over there are in the planes.
>
> We've played some of the toughest troops in the world and the guys have never been anything but courteous. Of course I know what they're thinking but if you could be arrested for that, this war would be taking place in Leavenworth.

The typical Hope show menu has never allowed the active GI imagination to go uninspired. Some of the most beautiful female stars in Hollywood have joined with Hope, to help entertain the troops.

Joey Heatherton, Frances Langford, Doris Day, Zsa Zsa Gabor, Anita Bryant, Jayne Mansfield, Dorothy Lamour, Marilyn Maxwell, Lana Turner, Raquel Welch and Carroll Baker have been some of the spoils of war.

In their various routines with Hope, the intellectual aspect of their appeal, if any, becomes secondary, and they are shown as strictly female females.

Hope becomes the mind of the GI's.

His quips and wisecracks originate from the same frame of

reference as theirs. His jokes may be subtler than theirs would be, but the intent and the effect are the same.

For those stars whose assets are strictly physical, Hope requires little more than facetious responses to his statements to provide a lively exchange and provoke the laughs.

The following routine with Carroll Baker in 1965 in Vietnam illustrates the technique:

Hope: (*Pointing to the audience*) How do you like this group of tigers, huh?

Baker: Oh, they make a beautiful sight. It looks like one big dessert tray.

Hope: Yeah. That's been left out in the sun too long. Carroll, you're considered the sexiest gal in movies today, isn't that so?

Baker: Bob, my pictures aren't meant to be that sexy. It's all in the mind.

Hope: It is, huh. (*To audience*) You're all under arrest! (*Back to Baker*) I loved you in *Harlow*. I've never seen such sexy and revealing gowns.

Baker: I was a little hoarse when I made that movie, didn't you notice?

Hope: I didn't even know it was a talkie:

Baker: Bob, how is it we've never been in a picture together?

Hope: Oh, I think the Code only allows one sex symbol at a time.

In addition to the beautiful girls, Hope's troupes usually have included prominent stars from the sports world.

GI's welcome the sight of heroes whose exploits they've read about or heard about on radio. One of the earliest sports personalities to make a trip with Hope was Billy Conn, the prizefighter from Pittsburgh, who joined the troupe in 1945.

Since that time, Hope has introduced the GI's to some of the most memorable names in the sports world, including Mickey Mantle, Johnny Bench, Vida Blue, Ben Hogan, Jimmy Demarest, Sam Snead, Arnold Palmer and Rafer Johnson.

He prefers to sign up guys who have had a great year and who have had a lion's share of news ink. It helps to make the troops feel that stateside life has not skipped them during the twelve months they are gone.

And he directs his stable of writers to tailor the particular star's skit script to his personality—country boy to swinger to offseason stockbroker.

226

Bob interviewing a wounded GI during one of his tours

In 1956, for instance, every trooper worth his barracks sports-talk knew that Mr. Baseball was outfielder and Triple Crown winner Mickey Mantle.

The hardnosed, obsessed baseball buffs also knew Mickey could hit like hell by day and swing like hell at night.

In this skit, performed during a tour that year of bases in Alaska, Hope played a tough veteran topkick (first sergeant). Mantle was a raw farmboy replacement. Another troupe-member played the part of a colonel concerned about reports Hope was being too tough on the men. The scene is the squad bay, a quonset hut.

Colonel: Sergeant, dismiss the men, I want to talk to you.

Hope: All right, men—you've got a ten minute break. Fall out, on the double, police the area, pick up the butts, polish the rocks, cut the grass and let's get some clean dirt on that lawn ... (*The men exit*) ... What did you wanna see me about, Colonel?

Colonel: THAT'S what I want to see you about ... Sergeant, you're riding the men too hard—you're not treating them like human beings.

Hope: But they're SOLDIERS! I only go accordin' to the book.

Colonel: The book's been changed. Your technique was all right in the old army ... But Washington has instituted a whole new policy. Gentleness, kindness, understanding, love ... that's what makes soldiers ...

Hope: Well, if you're talking about Wac's, yeah!

Colonel: I've got a new replacement outside—and if I get one complaint from this youngster about your treatment—I'll have your stripes.

Hope: But Colonel, I can't coddle the men in my platoon.

Colonel: Don't think of it as a platoon, think of it as a brood ... And you're the mother hen!

(*Colonel exits ... Gestures to Mickey Mantle, who steps in to applause*)

Hope: Welcome to the nest! (*Hope walks around the new man inspecting him disdainfully and then reads from a large tag fixed to his shirt pocket button*) ... "Michael Mantle. If lost return to J. D. Mantle, General Delivery, Commerce, Oklahoma. Return postage guaranteed." (*To Corporal, who is standing nearby*) He wasn't inducted—he was MAILED into the army! ... Michael Mantle.

Mantle: Yes, sir ... (*a very broad country boy grin*) Are you the Headmaster?

Hope: No, I'm the Housemother! (*Turns to Corporal*) Fix him up a tent on the target range.

Bob and Johnny Bench, the National League's Most Valuable Player in 1970, during the Christmas tour of the same year

Corporal: Sarge—remember your stripes ... Friendly, friendly.

Hope: Yeah ... (*Turns to Mantle*) Welcome to Blackhole ...

Mantle: That's mighty friendly of you ... (*Bites off chaw from tobacco plug, hands it to Hope*) Have a chaw.

Corporal: (*Pleased*) Well at least he chews tobacco.

Hope: Tobacco? This is a tootsie roll! (*Puts it in Mantle's pocket and asks gruffly*) Where's your papers?

Mantle: Right here, Mr. Sergeant. (*Hope checks them and then asks*)

Hope: What's this? (*Holds up a sheet of paper*)

Mantle: A note from my mother.

Hope: (*Reading*) "This is to introduce my son Michael. He is still a growing boy and needs his rest so do not wake him up too early in the morning. When you squeeze his orange juice make sure you strain the pits and the pulp. If he gets tired of his cod-liver oil sneak it into a malted milk." (*Hope glares*)

Mantle: You can forget about the cod-liver oil—I won't tell her. (*Hope pinches his cheek and slaps him fondly*)

Hope: Good boy. (*Reads again*) "He is inclined to be forgetful so be sure he has a clean handkerchief when you take him out for a walk." What've we got here—a soldier or a cocker spaniel? (*Reads*) "When he is getting dressed in the morning don't help him tie his shoelaces as he has been doing it by himself for almost a year now."

Hope: (*Pinching Mantle's cheek again*) Good boy! (*Reads*) "Let me know if he is not behaving himself and I will come and take him right home."

(*Hope grabs a .45 from holster on bed and cocks it*)

Corporal: (*Alarmed*) Sarge—what are you doin'?

Hope: I'm gonna kill it before it spreads!

Corporal: (*Grabs pistol*) Sarge—you can't—thirty years you worked for them stripes—you're not going to throw all that away ...

Hope: You're right ... (*To Mantle*) Okay—come on.

Mantle: Oh ... you gonna show me to my room?

Hope: (*Stopping suddenly*) It isn't ready yet ... We're having it redecorated ... Conrad Hilton checked out this morning and left a terrible mess. Temporarily you'll have to share this suite with us.

Mantle: Oh ... May I have the key?

Hope: The key!!!

Mantle: In case I stay out late I wouldn't want you to have to get up and open the door for me. (*Hope turns to the Corporal*)

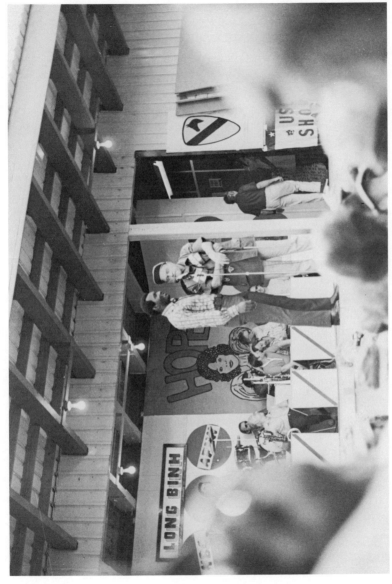

Bob exchanging quips with Vida Blue, the American League's Cy Young Award winner of 1971, during the Christmas tour of the same year

(*This time the Corporal hands him the .45*)

Hope: (*Pushes it away*) No, that's the easy way. (*To Mantle*) There's your bed, unpack your gear. Breakfast is at 0700.

Mantle: Yes, sir—what street?

Hope: (*Pinches his cheek, slaps him fondly*) Now I know what Stengel [the Yankee manager] goes through. Unpack!

Mantle: Yes sir.

(*Mantle opens barracks bag, takes out toilet article kit, shirts, underwear, puts them on footlocker. Next he takes out rolled up rug on floor beside bed. Takes boudoir lamp out of bag, Puts lampshade on it next to bed, plugs it in. Takes out bunny slippers, sets them on rug. Takes out set of pretty lace curtains on strings, fastens them on window. Steps back to admire his handiwork*)

Hope: Who drafted you—*Good Housekeeping*? (*Points to curtains*) Get that garbage out of here. You can't hang curtains in my barracks.

Mantle: Why not?

Hope: It clashes with the wallpaper in the washroom!

Mantle: (*Starts to walk away*) Maybe I better get the Colonel's permission. (*Hope grabs him, his attitude changes completely*)

Hope: Wait a minute—it does lend a certain air of enchantment.

Mantle: Then you *do* like it?

Hope: It's rather chic in a nauseating sort of way. (*Mantle pinches Hope's cheek, slaps it playfully*)

Mantle: You old Grizzly Bear, you. Your bark is worse than your bite. (*He turns away*) (*The Corporal has to restrain Hope*)

Corporal: Sarge—what are you gonna do?

Hope: I'm gonna bite him and show him how strong he is! (*Mantle yawns and stretches and turns to Hope*)

Mantle: I had a rough day—I think I'll turn in.

Hope: Fine. Why don't you do that? Get undressed.

Mantle: In front of everybody! (*Starts walking out again*)

Hope: Where are you going?

Mantle: I'm gonna see the Colonel ... about a dressing room.

Hope: You don't need the Colonel ... Corporal—his dressing room. (*Corporal takes blanket from bed and passes one end to Hope; both look away discreetly*)

Corporal: What are we gonna do when we're out on maneuvers?

Hope: One thing at a time ... We'll think of something—we'll build
– him a portable foxhole.

Corporal: Who's gonna break it to him that there are thirty-two other guys sharing this boudoir?

Hope: Oh! they'll have to go ... Listen, I've had enough of this—(*He drops blanket to reveal Mantle wearing a pair of Dr. Denton longjohns monogrammed "MM." On back is his batting average, .351*)

Corporal: Sarge, look—monogrammed Dr. Denton's. (*Mantle turns and reveals batting average*)

Hope: (*Hope points to it*) Up here, that's your salary for the year! (*Nurse enters, talking*)

Nurse: You got a new recruit in here? (*Mantle shyly covers up with the blanket*)

Hope: That's him—September Morn. (*Nurse looks at Mantle*)

Nurse: At ease ... (*to Hope*) he's gotta get his shots.

Mantle: I'll see you later. I've gotta talk to the Colonel.

Hope: (*Grabs him*) What do you need the Colonel for?

Mantle: Well ... I'm afraid of shots ... At home when I'm scared to take medicine, Mom takes a spoonful first just to show me it don't hurt.

(*All turn to Hope, who rolls up his sleeve to reveal service stripes all the way up his bare elbow. The nurse stares at them and then looks questioningly at Hope*)

Hope: We need discipline in the showers, too!

Nurse: I'll leave the matter in your hands, Sergeant. (*Puts hypo on bed and leaves*)

Hope: (*To Mantle*) Come here, you.

(*He pushes Mantle down on footlocker and rolls up his sleeve*)

Hope: You're gonna get your shot if it's the last thing I do. (*To Corporal*) Now give me the shot. (*He sits on the hypo*) Never mind, I GOT it!

(*He gets up*) Oh, what's the use ... Go on, Soldier—hit the sack. (*He starts to leave*)

Mantle: (*In a hurt tone*) Sarge—you mean you're not gonna tuck me in.

(*Hope stops in his tracks ... Crosses back to him ... Puts his arm around him and nods to Corporal, who starts playing "My Buddy" on harmonica as Colonel enters unnoticed*)

Hope: (*Over music*) Look, kid, I'm your pal ... I've been in the army a long time ... I know what it's like for a kid like you away from home the first time ... The loneliness, the need for friendship ... I wouldn't steer you wrong ... I'm gonna give you some good advice ...

(*Song ends*)

Hope: Why don't you desert???

(*The Colonel starts*)

Hope: Go over the hill—I'll never tell anybody ...

Mantle: What about the Colonel?

Hope: Old Yellowstain?? He hasn't been out of the sack in two years!

Colonel: Tenshun! (*Hope is startled when he sees the Colonel*)

Hope: Anyone for the firing squad????

Mantle: I don't feel so good. I think I'll lie down.

(*Mantle gets into bed*)

Colonel: (*To Hope*) I warned you that the new soldiers are to be treated with kindness and understanding—didn't I—*Private* Hope?

Hope: A private? After thirty years, sir—you're taking away my rank?

Colonel: That's right! You'll get no different treatment than any other new recruit.

Hope: Well, I'm glad to hear that (*Climbs into bed with Mantle*)

Colonel: What do you think you're doing?

Hope: (*Hands him a comic book*) Read us to sleep, Mother!

The skit's broad humor was a smash hit with the bored and holiday-season-glum servicemen sitting out a winter of discontent as pointmen in the continental defense network set up against a Russian sneak attack.

The cold war was going full blast. Khrushchev's faceoff with JFK in Cuba was still six years away.

As outrageous as the skit was as a description of service life and routine then, it also was equally prophetic about future military life.

With the exception of the U.S. Marine Corps, the Armed Forces in 1972 underwent a dramatic transformation. Almost overnight the once Spartan existence became a military love-in, with the old ways abandoned in an impassioned courtship by the brass of the new breed. The draft had been junked for a lottery system, and the chances of getting a letter from Washington that begins, "Greetings," dropped sharply.

The new GI reflected the society from which he was recruited. Like that society his tastes in entertainment had changed.

There was widespread suggestion that perhaps Hope was not as appealing to the latter-day GI as he was to his older brother or even

234

Bob kidding a GI during his tour of Korea in 1962

his father.

That perhaps Hope's double-entendre jokes about sex and single girls would lose their edge in front of a generation among whom premarital sex was as common as teething.

That perhaps Bob would be a big bore to troops on the nod from pot, passing a year involved in a war that everyone wanted ended—either with honor or without.

But Hope didn't become a service institution and a superstar by not changing with the times. One of his most valuable assets has been his ability to sense what his audience wants.

His Christmas tour of 1970 to Vietnam proved once again that maybe the critics had missed their target.

Hope's reception was reported by Sergeant John Mueller in an article that appeared in the December 24, 1970, issue of the *Pacific Stars and Stripes*:

"Hope arrived amid speculation that the 67-year-old show business veteran had lost his appeal among the younger GI's.

"But at the conclusion of Tuesday's performance, he received a wildly enthusiastic standing ovation from 18,000 troops who saw his first Vietnam show of the tour," Mueller wrote.

It was the same old Hope with some new material. Booze jokes were replaced with a rapid-fire patter about pot, the membership card of the liberated generation.

His comment, "I hear you fellows are interested in gardening. Our CO tells us you grow a lot of grass," turned the troops on.

This first allusion to the weed became more pointed in a later quip.

"Instead of taking it [pot] away from the soldiers we should be giving it to the negotiators in Paris," Hope joked. Wild applause and the realization that Hope wasn't brass like "they" said. He was EM, enlisted man all the way.

A reference to pot again appeared in a skit with Johnny Bench, acclaimed at the end of his first spectular season to be potentially the greatest catcher who ever lived. Bench was the National League's Most Valuable Player in 1970.

Bench, playing the straight man, remarked how much he enjoyed playing baseball. Hope's rejoinder was: "Where else can you play eight months on grass and not get busted?" Wild applause.

At a press conference following the show, Hope admitted that it was the first time he had used material about drugs.

"It's a real hot topic with the kids," he explained.

A typical audience of GI's waiting for Hope's entrance during his tour of South Vietnam in 1969

The rest of the show stuck to a success formula based on more than twenty-five years of experience entertaining troops. The cast included: Les Brown and his band, a regular feature; sports figures; and the women, as usual a talented and beautiful lineup—Lola Falana, a sultry dancer; Bobbie Martin, a country and western singer; Jennifer Hosten, Miss World, 1971.

Also, Gloria Loring, another singer; Ursula Andress, a stunning actress; and two chorus lines of curves from the "Dean Martin Show," the Goldiggers and the Dingalings.

It all added up to two and half hours of skits, songs, gags and sex. The perfect way for a rifleman to forget for a brief time where he was, why he was where he was and how many days he had left to worry about staying alive.

The preparation for a Hope Christmas jaunt begins early in the fall. The military authorities usually devise the schedule, with suggestions from Hope himself about bases to play. Hope has high-ranking friends and he likes to fill their requests.

It is not unusual for various parts of the itinerary to be kept secret for security reasons until the evening before a performance. Hope has joked about the frantic last-minute behind-the-scenes arrangements.

"Each summer the Joint Chiefs of Staff gather with the USO and commiserate," Hope once recounted jokingly. "He got back okay last Christmas. Okay, let's try harder," was his report on the top-level meeting.

He continued: "Then they drop little pieces of paper listing all the world's trouble spots into a hat and humming choruses from *Macbeth*, they stir gently."

By the middle of November, Hope has a definite idea of his destinations. Two advance men, Johnny Pawlek, chief sound engineer, and Silvio Caranchini, top assistant for television, visit the various bases scheduled for shows on a reconnaissance mission.

Their survey is concerned with logistics, equipment and facilities. Does the base have an engineering capability to build a stage? Are there quarters to house the performers? Is there a generator or an electrical plant for the mikes, lights and amplifiers?

Meanwhile, Hope has assembled the troupe. They undergo the paperwork involved in a security clearance. They bare their arms and grit their teeth for the long series of innoculations—shots for cholera, typhoid, typhus and so on.

Hope's writers are creating skits written around props that are

Bob embarking for one of his Christmas tours to Vietnam

simple and thus portable. The sets are not elaborate. Usually the girls are the scenery mainstay.

Barney McNulty prepares the idiot cards for Hope's monologues. Based on intelligence reports from Pawlek and Caranchini, his opening jokes consist of specific references to each base, its commanding officer and recent events in and out of combat.

Since the typical tour covers at least ten bases, the cards are vital.

The television technicians are recruited. It is interesting to note that along with the Hope regulars (Les Brown and Jerry Colonna), the TV crew also is composed of many professionals who have volunteered to make this trip before. These men celebrate Christmas with their families in January when they return.

The Department of Defense, which is funded by the taxpayer, provides the transportation for the tour. Hope's television sponsor absorbs the cost of filming the show.

Of late this arrangement has met with criticism and speculation about the altruistic validity of Hope's commitment to the troops. Since he derives so many benefits (free and continuous publicity, for example), the non-believers wisecrack that the whole fling is strictly financial.

His sponsor, of course, pays him for the show, which is considered one of his "specials" for the year.

The Christmas show itself repeatedly has been rated the Number-1 draw of the entire year—61 percent in 1971. That alone garners Hope even more publicity.

Before Hope's critics proceed to castigate him for exploiting the servicemen, they should consider the following.

He hardly could have anticipated the resultant success of the tour. Further, he was a star before the Christmas show became the institution it is today. And finally, when one appreciates the grueling conditions under which Hope works during the tour, and considers that he is fully capable of pulling down an equivalent amount of money doing less hectic stateside stints, the full value of Hope's gesture becomes credible.

No doubt he enjoys, even savors, the kudos and adulation that precede, accompany and follow a tour. In that regard, he's only typical of showmen the world over. Criticize that need and you are ripping off human nature.

The tour departs late in December from Travis Air Force Base north of San Francisco. The 1965 trip was fairly typical.

From touchdown at Wake Island to liftoff at Guam twelve days

This shy serviceman sings "You're Just Too Wonderful" to Miss World with the encouragement of Bob Hope during his 1966 tour of Vietnam

and 288 hours later, the routine was strictly nonstop with danger never farther away than the maximum range of a Viet Cong mortar round or ground-launched rocket.

The flight manifest contained the names of sixty-three cast and crew. Along with Hope and Les Brown and the band were singers Jack Jones, Anita Bryant and Kaye Stevens, actress Carroll Baker, nightclub star Joey Heatherton and, "don't say a word, just let us stare at you" Diana Lynn Batts, Miss USA.

In twelve days, 288 hours, the caravan flew 23,000 miles, crossing the international date line twice. They did twenty-four shows. Most were scheduled. Some were impromptu, shortened and performed for troops who had missed the main show.

First Day, December 20

After a twelve-hour flight from Travis AFB, touchdown at Wake Island and the first two-and-one-half-hour show. A meal and then takeoff for a twenty-two-hour flight to Bangkok.

Second Day, December 21

Bangkok show, morning. Noon show at Udon. This air base is located close to Laotian border. Stage built atop a sea of fifty-gallon fuel drums containing high octane aviation fuel. Mortar attacks an everyday hazard here, but this day the 2,500 men in the audience don't have their minds on their work. Lunch. Evening show at Ta Khil deep in the jungle, which is home to the king cobra, the most poisonous reptile in the world.

Third Day, December 22

Ubon, 225 miles north of Bangkok, Khorat, famed for the red hot red-light district outside the base, Camp Usarthai. Hope quips to the audience of 4,200: "Here we are at Khorat ... where Suzie Wong got her basic training." Later, Hope falls off the makeshift stage. His fall is broken by a security man, and he is not injured. The afternoon show is followed by a party at the Royal Thai palace hosted by the king and queen.

Fourth Day, December 23

Back to Bangkok to Don Muang Airport. Hope quips about fall to an audience of 5,000: "Actually, it was heat prostration. I black out every time I stand close to Carroll Baker." That evening a show aboard a Royal Thai Navy ship.

Hope sharing the spotlight with the Goldiggers during his Christmas tour of 1970

243

Fifth Day, December 24

A 400-mile flight to Saigon's Tan Son Nhut airport and two shows, which are a relief after the combat approach and landing. The plane drops from 6,000 feet (out of hostile small arms ground-fire range) to the runway in less than a minute. A press conference is held, followed by a show for 5,000. Then another briefer show at the Third Field Hospital. Dinner. Midnight mass. Hope isn't Catholic. His wife, Dolores is.

Sixth Day, December 25

Dian. The heat, 100 degrees, and the humidity, near 100 percent, are crushing, but 3,200 combat troops get a laugh out of Christmas Day, a way of life and world away from home. Before the show begins, a chilling announcement is made over the public address system.

"I want you men to keep the aisle clear on both sides of the stage. In case of mortar attack, the left side of the audience will move out the left, and the right side will move out to the right. The center section will move out to the rear. And the cast of the Bob Hope show will take cover in those cozy foxholes immediately adjacent to the stage." Bien Hoa. Ninety-eight degree heat and a combat-weary audience of 7,000 men. This base is the first hit by attacks at the end of the holiday truce.

Seventh Day, December 26

Cam Ranh Bay, a massive logistical base built on miles of white, shining sand 200 miles northeast of Saigon. During the show, a shot rings out. Heads flinch. Some men hit the deck. A Marine accidently had pulled the trigger on his M-73 grenade launcher. Quickly Hope retorts: "Everywhere you go, Red Skelton fans." A wild roar of laughter.

Eighth Day, December 27; Ninth Day, December 28

Helicopter flight to U.S.S. *Ticonderoga*, a carrier and the largest ship in the Sixth Fleet on Yankee Station in the South China Sea. Two days and two shows with most of the audience ferried aboard from other ships in the flotilla.

Tenth Day, December 29

An Khe, in the central highlands for a 10:50 A.M. show for over

Bob and Jennifer Hosten, Miss World, doing their rendition of "I Can Do Anything Better than You" during Bob's Christmas tour of 1970

10,000 troops. Flight of almost an hour to Nha Trang and a dinner show for 8,000.

Eleventh Day, December 30

No rest in the homestretch. Nine A.M. flight to Chu Lai, 200 miles, for a noon show. Chu Lai is leatherneck country and the grunts break up at Hope's opener: "I'm thrilled to be here in John Wayne land." John Wayne is a Marine film favorite, because he never dies, even in the withering Japanese fire in *The Sands of Iwo Jima*. At 2:55 P.M., 14:55 to the Marine pilots, the troupe flies north to Danang, to another Marine audience of 8,500. Flight out of Danang immediately after show ends to Clark Field, the Philippines. Audience of 3,000. Then a show at the hospital. Then still another show at the enlisted men's mess for the troops who missed the main show because they were on guard duty or other security assignment.

Twelfth Day, December 31

No sleep. Flight out of Clark AFB at 2 A.M. for the final stop, the nineteenth, at Gikeson Field, Guam. An audience of 20,000 sees this last two-and-one-half-hour performance at 3 P.M.

From the show at Nha Trang to the finale on Guam, the rest of the troupe found it hard to stand up. It is hard to believe, even for cynics, that only money is keeping them going. There are twenty-four straight hours of shows.

By Guam, some of the troupe are near a state of total collapse. However, Hope's fabled energy and drive keeps him well charged.

The work of the tour is not completed, even by touchdown in California. There are still 150,000 feet of film to be edited in time for the airing of the "Bob Hope Christmas Special," slated for viewing in mid-January.

Hope's final Christmas tour in 1972—a whirlwind 13-stop visit overseas to his loyal troops—ended at Anderson Air Force Base on Guam. Both America's longest war and Hope's 31-year career entertaining gobs, jarheads, airdales and dogfaces were drawing to a close.

Before he left the states, the comedian hinted he was thinking about not reenlisting for a hitch in 1973.

But at his first stop, Nam Phong, Thailand, he almost changed his mind. A spirited throng of 2,500 Marines, members of Air Group 15, bid Hope a spontaneous and highly emotional farewell. The young leathernecks sang a chorus of "Auld Lang Syne" and then swung into a rousing version of the "Marine Corps Hymn." It was as if they had sensed that they had just witnessed the end of a grand tradition.

However, some of the Thai newspapers were not quite as sentimental. They angrily declared that Hope's joke about the shaved heads of Buddhist monks resembling, from the air, a cantaloupe convention was disrespectful and irreverent. American ambassador Leonard Unger apologized for the slight by issuing a statement calling Hope "a friend of Thailand."

"He may not be familiar with Thailand's customs, but I am sure he would never purposely say anything to offend the Thai people," Unger stated.

Hope explained that he had not meant to hurt anyone. He said his only motive was "to generate laughter."

"I satirize, I exaggerate local customs in every country. I've been telling these jokes for 35 years," he declared.

Hope's last stop in South Vietnam was at Tan Son Nhut Air Base near Saigon. Next, the 78-member troupe, including comedian Redd Foxx, flew back to Bangkok. There, they caught a plane for a five hour 2,000-mile flight to Diego Garcia, a lonely outpost in the Indian Ocean manned by 1,000 seabees.

The coral isle is a worldwide communications station that at first glance seems like a lush tropical paradise. But for the troops, the novelty of the swaying palms and the soft sea winds wears off quickly, to be replaced by depression and boredom. The only exotic diversion, it seems, is watching exotic birds.

Hope's monologue struck deftly at the heart of the troop's opinion of their isolated retreat.

"Talk about remote," he cracked. "Only the Navy knows whether these guys are stationed here or marooned."

"I want to thank you for inviting us here—and the flies, for giving us permission to land," Hope joked.

Hope and company also played to a Navy audience on the sprawling flight deck of the carrier *Midway* anchored off Singapore. Half the ship's complement of 4,500 men elected to pass up the show and spend the day ashore taking in the sights and scents. One enlisted man who stayed aboard explained to a reporter that, "Nobody stays on board if they don't have to."

Another sailor, Reginald Garnett of Oakland, Cal., told why he had stayed to see the show.

"Bob Hope isn't really my kind of entertainer—I mean I like Redd Foxx's humor better. But still, Hope's the guy who gets these people over here and no matter what you think of him, politics or otherwise, you still have to admire the guy for going out of his way for us. I know I do. That's why I'm here," he said.

Hope has received numerous awards for his tireless efforts, including the Medal for Merit, presented on behalf of the government by General Dwight D. Eisenhower after World War II, and the Military Order of the Purple Heart.

But the less publicized and less glamorous testimonials are just as numerous, and, perhaps, even more meaningful. Some are quiet and rather shy nods of thank you by wounded vets, their eyes full of gratitude for the man who didn't forget them in their pain, sorrow and loneliness.

Others are letters such as this one on file with the USO.

It was sent by Mrs. John Gibson of Geneva, New York. Her grandson did a tour of duty in Korea as an MP. During Hope's 1970 Christmas visit, he was a security guard for the troupe.

Part of her note of appreciation was her personal thank you to Hope and the USO and a description of a letter her grandson sent to her.

Commenting on her grandson's letter, Mrs. Gibson said: "I believe it is a fine expression of general appreciation for the effort of Bob Hope and the USO program. It is particularly appropriate in view of the criticism leveled at both by some of the Jane Fonda-types who are obviously misled, naive, and gullible to the rantings of the malcontents roaming the countryside."

In her note Mrs. Gibson quoted an excerpt. It read as follows:

Ah, yes. The Bob Hope show. I had to stand behind to the right of the stage, so I didn't get to see the actual show too well. But I got a different kind of show.

I saw the girls shiver as they came out on the stage in the 15 degree weather in their scanty outfits. I saw Johnny Bench flexing his hands, trying to get the numbness out of his fingers as he came off the stage after his skits.

I saw Bob Hope alternately putting his hands behind him to flex his fingers. I saw the expressions on the GI's faces during the finale when everybody sang "Silent Night," and I saw a tear roll down Gloria Loring's cheek as she came backstage afterwards.

These are the little things you will never see on TV, but really add so much meaning to the whole thing.

But probably the greatest award of all for Hope is also the most intangible. It's not a medal, a trophy or a citation written in fancy script on a scroll. It's the memories of it all.

248

BOOKS BY BOB HOPE

☆ ☆ ☆ ☆ ☆ ☆ ☆ ☆ ☆ ☆ ☆ ☆ ☆ ☆ ☆

They Got Me Covered, 1941
I Never Left Home, 1944
So This Is Peace, 1946
Have Tux, Will Travel, 1954
I Owe Russia Twelve Hundred Dollars, 1963
Five Women I Love: Bob Hope's Vietnam Story, 1966

INDEX

(Page numbers in italics indicate
photographs of the referenced subjects)

254